New Dimensions in Public Utility Pricing

CONTEMPORARY STUDIES IN ECONOMIC AND FINANCIAL ANALYSIS, VOLUME 39

CONTEMPORARY STUDIES IN ECONOMIC AND FINANCIAL ANALYSIS

An International Series of Monographs

Series Editors: **Edward I. Altman and Ingo Walter**
Graduate School of Business Administration, New York University

Volume 1. **DYNAMICS OF FORECASTING FINANCIAL CYCLES: Theory, Technique and Implementation**
Lacy H. Hunt, II, *Fidelcor Inc. and the Fidelity Bank*

Volume 2. **COMPOSITE RESERVE ASSETS IN THE INTERNATIONAL MONETARY SYSTEM**
Jacob S. Dreyer, *Office of Monetary Research, U.S. Treasury*

Volume 3. **APPLICATION OF CLASSIFICATION TECHNIQUES IN BUSINESS, BANKING AND FINANCE**
Edward I. Altman, *Graduate School of Business Administration, New York University,* Robert B. Avery, *Graduate School of Industrial Administration, Carnegie-Mellon University,* Robert A. Eisenbeis, *Federal Deposit Insurance Corporation,* and Joseph F. Sinkey, Jr., *College of Business Administration, University of Georgia*

Volume 4. **PROBLEM AND FAILED INSITUTIONS IN THE COMMERCIAL BANKING INDUSTRY**
Joseph F. Sinkey, Jr., *College of Business Administration, University of Georgia*

Volume 5. **A NEW LOOK AT PORTFOLIO MANAGEMENT**
David M. Ahlers, *Graduate School of Business and Public Administration, Cornell University*

Volume 6. **MULTINATIONAL ELECTRONIC COMPANIES AND NATIONAL ECONOMIC POLICES**
Edmond Sciberras, *Science Policy Research Unit, University of Sussex*

Volume 7. **VENEZUELAN ECONOMIC DEVELOPMENT: A Politico-Economic Analysis**
Loring Allen, *University of Missouri, St. Louis*

Volume 8. **ENVIRONMENT, PLANNING AND THE MULTINATIONAL CORPORATION**
Thomas N. Gladwin, *New York University*

Volume 9. **FOREIGN DIRECT INVESTMENT, INDUSTRIALIZATION AND SOCIAL CHANGE**
Stephen J. Kobrin, *Sloan School of Management, Massachusetts Institute of Technology*

Volume 10. **IMPLICATIONS OF REGULATION ON BANK EXPANSION: A Simulation Analysis**
George S. Oldfield, Jr., *Graduate School of Business and Public Administration, Cornell University*

Volume 11. **IMPORT SUBSTITUTION, TRADE AND DEVELOPMENT**
Jaleel Ahmad, *Concordia University, Sir George Williams Campus*

Volume 12. **CORPORATE GROWTH AND COMMON STOCK RISK**
David R. Fewings, *McGill University*

Volume 13. **CAPITAL MARKET EQUILIBRIUM AND CORPORATE FINANCIAL DECISIONS**
Richard C. Stapleton, *Manchester Business and New York University,* and M.G. Subrahmanyam, *Indian Institute of Management and New York University*

Volume 14. **IMPENDING CHANGES FOR SECURITIES MARKETS: What Role for the Exchanges?**
Ernest Bloch and Robert A. Schwartz, *Graduate School of Business Administration, New York University*

Volume 15. **INDUSTRIAL INNOVATION AND INTERNATIONAL TRADING PERFORMANCE**
William B. Walker, *Science Policy Research Unit, University of Sussex*

Volume 16. **FINANCIAL POLICY, INFLATION AND ECONOMIC DEVELOPMENT: The Mexican Experience**
John K. Thompson, *Mellon Bank, N.A.*

Volume 17. **CORPORATE LIQUIDITY MANAGEMENT**
Michel Levasseur, *Centre d'Enseignement Superieur des Affaires, Jouy-en-Josas, France*

Volume 18. **STABILIZATION OF INTERNATIONAL COMMODITY MARKETS**
Paul Hallwood, *University of Aberdeen*

Volume 19. **PROBLEMS IN EUROPEAN CORPORATE FINANCE: Text and Cases**
Michel Schlosser, *Centre d'Enseignement Superieur des Affaires, Jouy-en-Josas, France*

Volume 20. **THE MULTINATIONAL ENTERPRISE: International Investment and Host-Country Impacts**
Thomas G. Parry, *School of Ecomomics, University of New South Wales*

Volume 21. **POLICY RESPONSES TO RESOURCES DEPLETION: The Case of Mercury**
Nigel Roxburgh, *Management Studies Division, The Economist Intelligence Unit, Ltd.*

Volume 22. **THE INTERNATIONAL MONEY MARKET: An Assessment of Forecasting Techniques and Market Efficiency**
Richard M. Levich, *Graduate School of Business Administration, New York University*

Volume 23. **TRANSNATIONAL CONGLOMERATES AND THE ECONOMICS OF DEPENDENT DEVELOPMENT: A Case Study of the International Electrial Oligopoly and Brazil's Electrical Industry**
Richard Newfarmer, *University of Notre Dame*

Volume 24. **THE POLITICAL ECONOMY OF ENVIRONMENTAL PROTECTION**
Horst Siebert, *University of Mannheim,* and Ariane Berthoin Antal, *International Institute for Environment and Society, Science Center, Berlin*

Volume 25. **BIDDING AND OIL LEASES**
James B. Ramsey, *New York University*

Volume 26. **THE ECONOMICS OF EXPLORATION FOR ENERGY RESOURCES**
James B. Ramsey, *New York University*

Volume 27. **TECHNOLOGY TRANSFER TO DEVELOPING COUNTRIES: The Case of the Fertilizer Industry**
Subrata Ghatak, *University of Leicester and University of Guelph*

Volume 28. **MULTINATIONALS: Bank and Corporation Relationships**
Olivier Pastre, *Universite Paris-Nord*

Volume 29. **THE PRIMARY MARKET FOR MUNICIPAL DEBT: Bidding Rules and Cost of Long-Term Borrowing**
G.O. Bierwag, *University of Oregon*

Volume 30. **EFFICIENCY IN THE MUNICIPAL BOND MARKET: The Use of Tax Exempt Financing for "Private" Purposes**
George G. Kaufman, *Loyola University of Chicago*

Volume 31. **FOREIGN INVESTMENT AND TECHNOLOGY TRANSFER: The Tire Industry in Latin America**
Peter West, *Caracus, Venezuela*

Volume 32. **DIMENSIONS OF ENERGY ECONOMICS**
Noel D. Uri, *Catholic University of America*

Volume 33. **INDIGENIZATION AND ECONOMIC DEVELOPMENT: The Nigerian Experience**
Nicholas Balabkins, *Lehigh University*

Volume 34. **INTERNATIONAL FINANCIAL MANAGEMENT: Problems, Issues, and Experiences**
John S. Oh, *Portland State University*

Volume 35. **PURCHASING POWER PARITY AND EXCHANGE RATES: Theory, Evidence and Relevance**
Lawrence H. Officer, *Michigan State University*

Volume 36. **FINANCIAL REPORTING RULES AND CORPORATE DECISIONS: A Study of Public Policy**
Bertrand Horwitz, *State University of New York-Binghamton* and Richard Kolodny, *University of Maryland*

Volume 37. **CONSUMER EMANCIPATION AND ECONOMIC DEVELOPMENT**
Hans B. Thorelli, *Villa Serbelloni, Bellagio and Indiana University* and Gerald D. Sentell, *NIDA, Bangkok and the University of Tennessee*

Volume 38. **INSURING NUCLEAR POWER: Liability, Safety and Economic Efficiency**
William C. Wood, *Owen Graduate School of Management, Vanderbilt University*

Volume 39. **NEW DIMENSIONS IN PUBLIC UTILITY PRICING**
Noel D. Uri, *Catholic University of America*

Volume 40. **ECONOMIC DECISIONS UNDER INFLATION: The Impact of Accounting Measurement Error**
Stephen M. Cross, *College of the Holy Cross*

To Gladys for her continued support

New Dimensions in Public Utility Pricing

by NOEL D. URI
Department of Economics and Business Administration
Catholic University of America

JAI PRESS INC.

Greenwich, Connecticut *London, England*

Library of Congress Cataloging in Publication Data

Uri, Noel D.
New dimensions in public utility pricing.

(Contemporary studies in economic and financial analysis; v. 39)
Includes bibliographical references and index.
1. Public utilities—Rates. I. Title. II. Series.
HD2763.U74 1983 363.6'068'8 81-81648
ISBN 0-89232-239-X

36 Sherwood Place
Greenwich, Connecticut 06836

JAI PRESS INC.
3 Henrietta Street
London WC2E 8LU
England

ISBN NUMBER: 0-89232-239-X
Library of Congress Catalog Card Number: 81-81648
Manufactured in the United States of America

CONTENTS

List of Tables

Preface

Growing demand, increasing cost and changing social values have combined to place increasing stress on the electrical energy industry. Recurrent and spreading power shortages are in the foreseeable future unless positive steps are taken to remedy conditions inhibiting the efficient development of generating capacity. Similarly, increasing prices for electrical energy seem to be the norm rather than the declining prices that have been the general experience of the past. Operation and maintenance costs and fuel costs are being forced up by market pressure at a faster rate than they are being offset by technological developments that reduce costs. Since the industry has a large base of imbedded capital investment which acts to dilute the increased cost of investment in new capacity and because of time lags in rate adjustment procedures, the cost increases of the past few years are just now being translated into rate increases.

It is already too late to circumvent further difficulties. Investment in new equipment cannot take place instantaneously so it will take time to correct inadequacies in generating capacity. Demand for electrical energy continues to grow unabated. In such a situation something must give and what has been yielding has been the level of reliability. Voltage reductions and a few localized blackouts have occurred in recent years when utilities were obliged to reduce or shed loads during peak demand periods to avoid overloading the system.

Within the context of these difficulties, opportunities exist for increasing the efficiency with which electrical energy is priced and allocated. Coincident with this is the realization that these activities constitute a continuous and sequential process involving the mobilization and efficient use of resources. The important aspect of these in the electrical energy sector is the formulation of suitable policies to carry out the economic activities of generating, pricing, and consuming over time and over space.

The tools of the economist are sufficiently well developed to investigate the problems mentioned above. It is hoped that, in a normative way, the recommendations will be considered by policy makers and in a positive way, the methodology will be closely scrutinized by the individuals responsible for investment decisions in the electrical energy industry. This last group, however, should temper their analysis with the realization that throughout this work, attention is concentrated on the basic economic aspects of the problem. It must be clearly understood that the discussion pays little attention to many aspects of practical engineering that necessarily loom large in the eyes of those who face the technical side of the problem.

Finally, the views expressed here are my own and do not necessarily represent the policies of the organizations with which I have been and currently am associated.

Chapter I

Introduction

INTRODUCTION

Considerations of the optimal pricing of public utility service arise from the inability to economically store the product produced and the temporal fluctuations in the demand for the product. In the case of electrical energy in the United States, the demand fluctuates by time of day and season of the year. It is typically the smallest in the winter and largest in the summer. This peak demand means that capacity has to exist to satisfy demand. Implicitly, some capacity is not utilized at other times, and this idleness (with the accompanying cost to an electric utility) is the basis of the optimal pricing problem (typically called the *peak-load pricing problem*).

The peak-load problem in electric utilities became transparent when electrical energy was used primarily for lighting. Daily peaks occurred at dusk when lights were turned on. Pricing principles were delineated to curb this peak demand. In fact, John Hopkinson suggested the use of maximum demand changes in the 1890s. The Hopkinson tariff—with a kilowatthour (kWh) charge as well as a charge per kilowatt (kW) of maximum demand—has since become the basis for electrical energy rate making.

The interest of economists in the peak-load pricing problem is a relatively recent phenomenon. Major early contributors included Boiteux,[1] Houthakker,[2] Little,[3] and Steiner.[4] The approach suggested was to base prices on marginal costs of production. By precisely equating the marginal costs with consumers' willingness to pay for additional output, a balance is achieved between the social costs of increasing production and the consumer satisfaction resulting from such an increased output. In addition to these equity considerations, marginal cost pricing has intraindustry efficiency advantages in that the determination of long-run marginal costs is forward looking in contrast to pricing based on recovery of historical accounting costs and consequently necessitates a rational evaluation of future trends in such matters as inflation and factor prices, and the electric utility's planned response to such trends. One consequence of marginal cost pricing is that peak-period consumers will have to pay a higher price than off-peak users since marginal increases in peak demand involve expanding capacity in the long run, whereas increased off-peak demand simply incurs incremental production costs (operating and maintenance costs including fuel costs) on existing units.

The standard approach to the peak-load problem has evolved from the work of Boiteux[5] and Steiner.[6] Both contain essentially the same solution. Because the formulation of the problem is slightly different between the two, only Steiner's will be highlighted. He adopted a welfare-maximizing approach first developed by Hotelling whereby prices are set to achieve the maximization of expressed consumer satisfaction over the cost of resources devoted to production. This is tantamount to assuming that an electric utility attempts to maximize welfare as measured by

$$\text{NSW} = \text{SB} - \text{SC} = \text{TR} + \text{CS} - \text{TC} \tag{1.1}$$

where NSW = net social welfare;
SB = social benefits;
SC = social costs;
TR = total revenue;
CS = consumers' surplus;
TC = total cost.

The net benefits to producers are clearly TR − TC. Net benefits to consumers are represented by consumers' surplus and are measured by the area under the usual Marshallian demand curve and above the price line. The welfare measure is neutral with respect to which group of consumers or producers benefit. Further, the welfare function considers only aggregate social benefits and costs and not the welfare of any specific group. The justification for this presumption is that public utilities should behave in general to achieve the maximum net benefit while relegating distributional considerations to other public policy instruments such as taxes. In this way the efficiency and distributional considerations of public utility planning are separated. If this assumption is made and the welfare function NSW is maximized, then prices should be set equal to marginal costs.

In doing this, Steiner assumes a typical day divided into two equal-length periods each possessing an independent demand curve. The peak-load pricing problem under consideration results from the assumption that one of the two demand curves lies everywhere above the other. The demands are independent in that the price charged in one period has no effect on the quantity demanded in the other. Costs are assumed to be linear: b is the operating cost per unit in each period, and β is the cost of adding an additional unit of capacity. This unit of electrical energy demanded in a period will cost b if the capacity exists to supply it and $b + \beta$ if capacity must be added. Once a unit of capacity has been installed (at cost β), it is available for meeting demands in both periods. Algebraically prices are set in the off-peak period at $p_1 = b$ with output X_1 and in the peak period at $p_2 = b + \beta$ with output X_2 such that $X_1 < X_2$ and $X_2 = q$, where q is the capacity.

In this instance, the peak period revenue p_2X_2 covers the identifiable peak period costs, both capacity (βq) and operating costs (bX_2) and the off-peak period revenue p_1X_1 covers only operating costs. Since it follows from the welfare formulation that no price is lower than b nor greater than $b + \beta$, charging the maximum feasible price in the peak period and the minimum feasible price in the off-peak period represents the extremes. Steiner suggests that to the extent these prices can be changed while still leaving spare capacity (i.e., $X_1 < q$) in the off-peak period, then such prices are optional.

In the foregoing case (called the *firm peak* case), one demand curve always was above the other. In a situation of a shifting peak, what was the off-peak demand (X_1) now becomes the larger quantity demanded and consequently is the determinant of the amount of capacity needed. This solution fails to maximize welfare. The correct solution is obtained by adding vertically the two demand curves. Where this aggregate demand curve cuts the horizontal line drawn at $2b + \beta$ (off-peak and peak) determines optimal capacity q allowing prices to be calculated from the individual demand curves. The sum of the off-peak and peak prices, $p_1 + p_2$, must equal, of course, $2b + \beta$. Peak users pay a higher price than off-peak users even though the quantity supplied is potentially the same.

In the situation of the shifting peak demand, both demands contribute to capacity cost (β), and capacity is fully utilized in both periods. There is no exact rule for allocating capacity costs between peak and off peak. It depends on the strengths of the demands. Thus, if peak demand increases relative to off-peak demand, optimality requires that consumers in the peak period pay a relatively larger share of the capacity cost. It is not only the relationship between the demands that determine whether it is a firm or shifting peak. The magnitude of the capacity cost relative to demand is also important. If capacity costs are relatively larger, any failure (e.g., as in the firm peak case) to fully use capacity is costly and encourages improved utilization or a change to a shifting peak.

The simple peak-load pricing problem has provided the basis for extensions that better approximate the realities faced by electric utilities. The assumptions have been made less restrictive. For example, Williamson[7] allows demand periods of unequal length, Mohring[8] incorporates increasing returns to scale, Uri[9] considers alternative plant types, and stochastic demands are incorporated by Brown and Johnson.[10] All of the solutions presented reinforce the Boiteux–Steiner results that, in principle, prices and technology should be chosen so that efficient generation of electrical energy results and so that there is an equilibration between what consumers are willing to pay and the social costs of additional output at the margin (i.e., marginal-cost pricing to the extent possible).

In sum, the theoretical literature has found under a variety of assumptions that prices based on marginal costs maximize the social welfare function.

Spatial Dimensions

These developments unfortunately neglect an important institutional characteristic. Namely, the electric utility industry is characterized by a spatial separation of supply (producers) and demand (consumers) and by a fixed amount of transmission capacity available at any given time joining the producers and consumers. Any consideration of the optimal pricing of public utility service must incorporate this dimension.

As with the literature on peak-load pricing, the theoretical literature on spatial diffusion is very rich. Almost 30 years ago, Stephen Enke[11] considered in a purely descriptive framework how one good would be traded among several spatially separated markets. He argued that by assuming regions are separated but not isolated by a volume-dependent transportation cost per physical unit, assuming that there are no legal restrictions to limit the actions of the profit-seeking traders of each region, assuming that for each region the functions relating to local production and local use are given, and assuming that transportation cost is known, one can ascertain (1) the net price in each region; (2) the quantity of exports or imports for each region; (3) which regions export, import, or do neither; and (4) the volume and direction of trade between all possible regions.

Samuelson[12] considered this spatial problem, casting Enke's descriptive formulation mathematically into a maximum problem and related this specification to a standard problem in linear programming, the so-called Koopmans–Hitchcock minimum-transport-cost problem. Samuelson then suggested that after the problem in descriptive price behavior has been converted into a maximum problem, it can be solved by trial and error or by a systematic procedure of varying shipments in the direction of increasing net social welfare (NSW).

Takayama and Judge[13] restated the Samuelson partial-equilibrium (one commodity) formulation disregarding the interdependencies with other commodities and concentrating on the interdependencies that exist between the different markets in the production, pricing, and use of the one commodity. This is accomplished by postulating appropriate linear dependencies between regional supply, demand, and price and converting the Enke-Samuelson specification into a quadratic programming problem. The existence of aggregate linear regional demand and supply relations are assumed. The formulation was restated by Takayama and Woodland[14] clarifying the relationship between various price and quantity formulations. The problem was stated in its primal and "purified" dual form, i.e., entirely in terms of either price variables or in terms of quantity variables.

Noting that economic relations in time have many of the properties of economic relations in space, Samuelson[15] in subsequent work discussed the problem of intertemporal price equilibrium and suggested how the tools for analyzing spatial competitive relations might be applied to the more complex problems of equilibrium commodity prices over time. This problem is much more complex because the theory is inextricably bound up with uncertainty.

Operating with these considerations, Takayama and Judge[16] extend their spatial formulation to obtain the competitive price and product allocation when markets are separated by both space and time. In particular, the concept of net social welfare is used as a basis for deducing the conditions of spatial and intertemporal equilibrium; and given linear dependencies between regional supply, demand, and price for each time period and given transportation cost among regions and storage cost from time period t to time period t + 1, the problem is converted into a quadratic programming problem that can be solved directly for a competitive solution.

Qualification

Although many of the problems of determining the optimal pricing of public utility service across utilities in various sectors is the same, there are also significant differences among sectors as a result of product and technology differences. To be concrete, the electric utility industry will be focused on. Further, the development is not cast in a general equilibrium framework. Other markets are considered to be outside of the investigation.

This implies that certain unknowns are taken as given and due to this ceteris paribus assumption, a simplified or partial equilibrium situation is faced that is defined as a price equilibrium. If it turns out that these other markets do not fulfill the optimality conditions (see, e.g., Henderson and Quandt[17]), then globally the allocation and pricing of electrical energy resulting might not be efficient. Consequently, be cautioned that when the concept of efficiency is discussed, it is in this partial equilibrium setting.

The allocation that will lead to increased efficiency rests on the normative formulation of the problem. The models used normatively show how the output of electrical energy at many locations should flow to many consuming areas if optimal conditions are to be attained and costs minimized. If one is to produce quantitative statements describing the existing markets and predict the future course of economic variables (positive economics), a positive model is required. From the positive economics point of view, an optimal pricing model is an economic model in which the economic system may be described by a set of simultaneous equations including aggregate demand for each good by consumers for each market, the aggregate supply of each good by producers for each market, the distribution activities over space, and equilibrium conditions. If a simultaneous solution of an exogenously estimated structural equation was intended as a positive analysis, it would be subject to Haavelmo's[18] criticism. Unfortunately, a model of the electrical energy sector does not lend itself to this simultaneous system approach, and hence the models developed must be interpreted in a normative sense.

A methodological note should be inserted at this point. Many of the models formulated in the ensuing chapters rest on this notion of net social welfare—consumers' plus producers' surplus less total transport cost and total storage cost. A rejection of the viability of the economic surplus concept of necessity, it may be argued, leads to a rejection of the entire peak-load pricing framework as developed by Takayama and Judge and Steiner. The arguments for and against the economic surplus concept are long and heated (see Currie, Murphy, and Schmitz[19]). It is not the purpose here to attempt any justification for the use of the concept. It is simply observed that while it is easy to raise objections to the use of the concept of economic surplus, it is difficult to find any workable alternative.

As a final comment on the methodology adopted, observe

as Bhagwati[20] has stressed, that the measurement of losses and gains from changes in policy has resulted from pressure on economists to provide such measures. Policies are maintained or changed largely for noneconomic reasons; though the magnitude of the (economic) cost involved is commonly demanded and considered in discussions of public policy. Whether one likes it or not, this is what the decision-maker wants. In consonance with the best traditions in the profession, the theorist has begun to meet this need in an attempt to bring economic analysis closer to fulfilling the objective that provides its ultimate reason for existence. The result has been a definite and significant trend toward measurement of welfare change.

Overview

The problem to be investigated is the optimal pricing of public utility service when consumers and producers are spatially diffuse. Various approaches to this issue are explored beginning with the simplest case of social welfare maximization with deterministic demands and ending with a profit-maximization objective where demands are stochastic. Because of the complexities of some of the problems, it is necessary to vary the notation and formulation from one setting to the next in order to make the problem mathematically tractable. Additionally, there is a tendency to become mentally lazy if the same terms and symbols are used repeatedly. Consequently, the reader is advised to approach each chapter as an independent entity, looking for the nuances present.

In what follows, Chapter II is concerned with the basic problem formulation of optimal pricing where, in the historical mold, the objective is to maximize social welfare. The subsequent chapter attempts to give some empirical content to these relationships by looking at the pricing of electrical energy for the United States in a planning context covering the period 1975 through 1990. Chapter IV introduces a different objective function. The implications of maximizing profit without and then with regulatory constraint are fully explored. One finds in Chapter V the application of some of the concepts where profit maximization is the objective. An issue of considerable interest recently has been the effect of environmental regulations (e.g., the limitation of the construction of nuclear generating plants in particular regions). Chapter VI fully explores these in both the welfare-maximization and profit-maximization cases. Considerable criticism has arisen because of the use of the normative concept of welfare maximization to suggest the nature of the optimal pricing of public utility service. Consequently, Chapter VII is devoted to taking a profit-maximization perspective, imposing efficiency constraints, and exploring the pricing implications. The assumptions in the first seven chapters all presuppose that demands in one period to the next are known with certainty or are available in the certainty-equivalent sense and that they are temporally independent. Chapter VIII addresses this latter issue, while Chapters IX and X address the former. The examination of the effect of stochastic demands on the optimal pricing of public utility service when reliability is introduced leads to some interesting conclusions. The final chapter (Chapter XI) endeavors to put all of the models developed into perspective while highlighting the elements of importance.

NOTES

1. M. Boiteux, "Peak Load Pricing." *Journal of Business 33*(April): 157–198, 1960.
2. H. S. Houthakker, "Electricity Tariffs in Theory and Practice." *Economic Journal 61*(March): 1–25, 1951.
3. I. M. D. Little, *The Price of Fuel.* New York: Oxford University Press, 1953.
4. P. O. Steiner, "Peak-Loads and Efficiency Pricing." *Quarterly Journal of Economics 71*(November): 585–610, 1957.
5. Boiteux, Op. Cit.
6. Steiner, Op. Cit.
7. O. D. Williamson, "Peak Load Pricing and Optimal Capacity." *American Economic Review 56*(September): 810–827, 1966.
8. H. Mohring, "The Peak Load Problem With Increasing Returns and Pricing Constraints." *American Economic Review 60*(September): 693–705, 1970.
9. N. D. Uri, *Towards an Efficient Allocation of Electrical Energy*. Lexington, Mass.: D.C. Heath, 1975.
10. G. Brown and M. B. Johnson, "Public Utility Pricing and Output Under Risk." *American Economic Review 59*(March): 119–129, 1969.
11. S. Enke, "Equilibrium Among Spatially Separated Markets, Solution by Electric Analogue." *Econometrica 19*(January): 40–47, 1951.

12. P. A. Samuelson's formulation is in his "Spatial Price Equilibrium and Linear Programming." *American Economic Review 42*(June): 283–303, 1952. This work draws on T. Koopman's discussion in *Activity Analysis of Production and Allocation.* New York: John Wiley & Sons, 1951, pp. 229–259 and pp. 359–373.
13. T. Takayama and G. G. Judge, "Equilibrium Among Spatially Separated Markets: A Reformulation." *Econometrica 32*(October): 510–524, 1964.
14. T. Takayama and A. D. Woodland, "Equilivance of Price and Quantity Formulations of Spatial Equilibrium: Purified Duality in Quadratic and Concave Programming." *Econometrica 38*(November): 889–906, 1970.
15. P. A. Samuelson, "Intertemporal Price Equilibrium: A Prologue to the Theory of Speculation." *Weltwirtschaftliches Archiv 79:* 181–221, 1957.
16. T. Takayama and G. G. Judge, "An Intertemporal Price Equilibrium Model." *Journal of Farm Economics 46*(May): 477–487, 1964.
17. J. Henderson and R. E. Quandt, *Microeconomic Theory,* 2nd, ed. New York: McGraw-Hill Book Company, 1971, pp. 255–264.
18. Haavelmo suspects that a most dangerous procedure in estimating parameters in a system of stochastic equations is to fit each equation separately without regard to the fact that the variables involved are usually assumed to satisfy, simultaneously, a number of other stochastic relations. T. Haavelmo, "The Statistical Implications of a System of Simultaneous Equations." *Econometrica 11*(January): 2, 1943.
19. The entire controversy is summarized in J. J. Currie, J. A. Murphy, and A. Schmitz, "The Concept of Economic Surplus and its use in Economic Analysis." *The Economic Journal 81*(December): 741–799, 1971.
20. J. Bhagwati, "The Pure Theory of International Trade: A Survey," by American Economic Association and Royal Economic Society, *Surveys of Economic Theory,* Volume 2, St. Martins Press, New York, 1965, p. 213.

Chapter II

Optimal Pricing of Public Utility Service under Welfare Maximization

INTRODUCTION

As noted previously, public utilities have been concerned for almost a century with determining philosophies and techniques of pricing where demand varies temporally (i.e., monthly, weekly, and hourly).[1] It should be clear, however, that a public utility may supply a product for which the demand varies other than with time. In this chapter the spatial dimension of demand is combined with the temporal dimension to yield an optimal price. Thus, what is to be considered is the variation in the demand and price for electrical energy over time produced at centrally located generating plants and transmitted and distributed to consumers at various distances.

The optimal capacity of the plant and the pricing of the utility services are dependent on the set of assumptions used to define the problem. Turvey[2] examines the most important of these assumptions and discusses the implications of removing them for electrical energy tariffs. One of these rests on the empirical observation that an electric utility production technique consists of employing plants that have different cost characteristics according to their role in meeting demand. Although Turvey does not explicitly state what are optimal prices when a firm uses more than one plant to meet its peak loads, he suggests that prices equal to marginal operation and maintenance cost (hereafter operating cost) are relevant. He is critical of the assumption of constant marginal operating cost and constant incremental capacity cost as being too simple to be meaningful. He notes that, for an electrical energy system consisting of plants of different vintage, location, and type and consequently operating cost, the system marginal operating cost curve is upward sloping. The consequence of this is that price equal to marginal operating cost in all off-peak periods will vary between these periods.[3] One of the issues investigated here is what are the relevant marginal-cost pricing decisions when it is possible to employ more than one plant to meet demand.

A second assumption examined by Turvey is that the demand for electrical energy in a period of the demand cycle is independent of the demand of every other period. While this assumption is clearly wrong, this dependence is not explicitly handled in the present study since it would needlessly complicate the picture. The approach that would be followed if dependent demand was included is outlined by Cicchetti and Jurewitz.[4]

A third basic assumption underlying the formulation of the peak-load pricing problem is that the demand functions for electrical energy are known with certainty or are available in a certainty-equivalence sense. Two implications of this assumption are that the division into periods presents no problems and that the demand curves are not stochastic. For example, the combination of variable weather with a significant use of electrical energy for either space heating or air conditioning introduces an important stochastic element into electrical energy demand since, in addition to the regular daily and seasonal variations of these loads, there are also variations due to short-term weather changes. Thus, prices should be varied to meet short-run fluctuations in demand functions induced by weather changes. Consumers, however, may prefer a simpler tariff which covers the cost of meeting a stochastically fluctuating demand. What they desire is both electrical energy and the right to use more if the weather changes for the worse. In general, the willingness of consumers to pay for supply security, subject to the technical configuration of the supply system (i.e., plant sizes relative to total capacity and so on), must be considered. Consequently, utilities provide a margin of spare capacity for occasional use. This means that expected demand is less than available capacity. The magnitude of this margin of spare capacity depends on how much consumers value the availability of a margin to provide for supply security. Here it will be assumed that this margin, call it δ, is constant across all plants for all time and is simply reflected by inflating the existing level of capacity appropriately.

Orientation

As a basis for the specification to follow, the problem of equilibrium among spatially and temporally separated markets is couched in terms of the underlying demand and supply relations and is defined as the sum of the areas under the demand functions less the sum of the areas under the supply functions at equilibrium prices. Further, it is necessary to introduce transmission costs to capture the spatial aspects of the problem and to introduce distribution costs to more accurately represent the cost side since it is more expensive to distribute electrical energy to some consumers than to others; e.g., it is more expensive to distribute electrical energy to residential consumers than to industrial consumers on the average.

ENVIRONMENT

Visualize an economy where there are many consumers of electrical energy and many generating plants each of which are spatially separated. To formulate the understanding and development of the model, the following definitions and notation are introduced:

Let $i = 1, 2, \ldots, N$ denote the consumers;
$j = 1, 2, \ldots, \theta$ denote the generating plants[5];
$t, \tau = 1, 2, \ldots, T$ denote the discrete time periods of equal length;
y_{ijt} = quantity of electrical energy demanded by consumer i from plant j in period t;
x_{jit} = quantity of electrical energy supplied by plant j to consumer i in period t;
x_{jt} = quantity of electrical energy generated by plant j in period t;

I_{jt} = investment in generating plant j that will be available for operation in period t;
$\hat{I}_{jt}$ = maximum possible investment in generating plant j in period t;
K_{j1} = generating capacity of plant j in period 1;
d_{jit} = delivery cost (including transmission and distribution costs) by plant j and distributed to consumer i in period t;[6]
α_{jt} = operating cost (including fuel cost) for plant j in period t;
β_{jt} = cost of capital for an additional unit of generating capacity for plant j in period t;[7]
r = rate of interest.

Relying on the assumption that the demand functions of each consumer for each time period are known with certainty or are available in the certainty equivalence sense, the demand functions are given in the following form:

$$P_{ijt} = g_{ijt}\,(y_{ijt}), \tag{2.1}$$

where P_{ijt} is the price of electrical energy to consumer i from plant j in period t. The implications of this assumption are discussed by Mohring.[8]

The search for optimum demands, prices, and operating schedules is subject to a number of constraints:

1. For each plant in each time period, the total quantity of electrical energy generated by a plant must be greater than or equal to the quantity demanded by all consumers from that plant:

$$y_{jt} \leq \sum_{i} x_{jit}, \tag{2.2}$$

where the total quantity of electrical energy demanded from plant j is the sum of the quantities demanded by all consumers:

$$y_{jt} = \sum_{i} y_{ijt}. \tag{2.3}$$

2. For each plant and each time period, the total generation

of electrical energy is greater than or equal to the quantity supplied by that plant to all consumers:

$$\sum_{i} x_{jit} \leq x_{jt}. \tag{2.4}$$

3. For each plant and each time period, total generation is less than or equal to the maximum capacity:

$$x_{jt} \leq K_{j1} + \sum_{\tau=1}^{t} I_{jt}. \tag{2.5}$$

   There is a temptation to include a term to account for the rate of decline in output over time due to "age." However, since it is not significant for well-maintained generating plants, the term is excluded. Further, if capacity is not added in period t or the plant does not exist in the initial period, I_{jt} or K_{j1} will be appropriately zero.

4. For each region, investment in generating capacity of a plant is constrained by physical, institutional, and technological limitations:

$$I_{jt} \leq \hat{I}_{jt}. \tag{2.6}$$

For example, it is well recognized that there is a maximum feasible expansion in, say, nuclear power development considering the constraints imposed by such things as licensing, development of additional uranium supplies, technical and construction manpower limitations, difficulties with new and extrapolated equipment, and so on.[9]

Before proceeding, a number of points need to be clarified concerning the economic environment:

1. Additions to capacity are looked upon as an average. To include a margin of spare capacity required to meet demands above the mean expectation, the I_{jt} can be inflated by the appropriate margin.
2. There is no discussion of terminal conditions. This does not preclude such discussions in a variant of the model.

3. The formulation is deterministic. Accounting for uncertainties in demand, plant availability, and so forth can be included in the margin of spare capacity factor.
4. Attention is focused on the basic economic aspects of the problem with no attention being paid to all sorts of practical engineering aspects. It must be recognized that this planning model use is the first of several stages of the investment decision process. The search for a solution that satisfies economic and engineering criteria is an iterative process.

A MODEL FOR OPTIMAL PRICING

It is now possible to form the total discounted net social welfare function NSW for the peak-load pricing model as follows:

$$W = \sum_{t} \sigma^{t-1} \left[\sum_{i} \sum_{j} \int g_{ijt}(y_{ijt})\, dy_{ijt} - \sum_{j} \alpha_{jt} x_{jt} - \sum_{j} \beta_{jt} I_{jt} - \sum_{i} \sum_{j} d_{jit} x_{jit} \right], \tag{2.7}$$

where $\sigma^{t-1} = \dfrac{1}{(1+r)^{t-1}}$.

Providing the demand functions are downward sloping, the objective function is concave, and the Kuhn–Tucker conditions will give the necessary and sufficient conditions for a competitive solution.[10]

Associate the dual variables $\sigma^{t-1}\lambda_{1jt}$, $\sigma^{t-1}\lambda_{2jt}$, $\sigma^{t-1}\lambda_{3jt}$, $\sigma^{t-1}\lambda_{4jt}$ with constraints (2.2), (2.4), (2.5), and (2.6). Multiplying through by σ^{t-1} where appropriate, the Kuhn-Tucker conditions are

$$y_{jt} \le \sum_{i} x_{jit} \qquad \lambda_{1jt} \ge 0 \tag{2.8}$$

$$\sum_{i} x_{jit} \le x_{jt} \qquad \lambda_{2jt} \ge 0 \tag{2.9}$$

$$x_{jt} \le K_{j1} + \sum_{\tau=1}^{t} I_{jt} \qquad \lambda_{3jt} \ge 0 \tag{2.10}$$

$$I_{jt} \le \hat{I}_{jt} \qquad \lambda_{4jt} \ge 0 \tag{2.11}$$

$$g_{ijt}(y_{ijt}) \leq \lambda_{1jt} \qquad y_{ijt} \geq 0 \tag{2.12}$$

$$\lambda_{1jt} \leq d_{jit} + \lambda_{2jt} \qquad x_{jit} \geq 0 \tag{2.13}$$

$$\lambda_{2jt} \leq \alpha_{jt} + \lambda_{3jt} \qquad x_{jt} \geq 0 \tag{2.14}$$

$$\sum_{t' \geq t} \sigma^{t'-t} \lambda_{3jt} \leq \beta_{jt} + \lambda_{4jt} \qquad I_{jt} \geq 0. \tag{2.15}$$

λ_{3jt} can be interpreted as the quasi-rent of plant j in period t and, if that plant is utilized, is equal to the supply price minus marginal operating cost. Thus, if $x_{jt} < 0$,

$$\lambda_{3jt} = \lambda_{2jt} - \alpha_{jt}. \tag{2.16}$$

Suppose, in addition, $y_{ijt} > 0$ and $x_{jit} > 0$. To minimize total cost, production will be scheduled on equipment in increasing order of operating cost and delivery cost. Therefore, the demand price to a consumer in period t equals the distribution and transmission costs plus operating cost on the least efficient plant, denoted by j*, being used to generate electrical energy. Thus, if

$$0 < x_{j^*t} < K_{j^*t} + \sum_{\tau=1}^{t} I_{j^*t},$$

$$\text{then } g_{ij^*t}(y_{ij^*t}) = \alpha_{j^*t} + d_{j^*it}. \tag{2.17}$$

The quasi-rent of any plant j in use is equal to the difference between its operating cost plus distribution cost plus transmission cost and these costs accounted for by the least efficient plant. Thus, if

$$x_{jt} > 0, \qquad \lambda_{3jt} = \alpha_{j^*t} + d_{j^*it} - (\alpha_{jt} + d_{jit}). \tag{2.18}$$

Observe that it is possible to use a plant to generate electrical energy that does not have the lowest operating cost. If the transmission cost is sufficiently large, then it might be optimal to use a plant with a higher operating cost while shutting down a more efficient one.

Additions to capacity are undertaken on the basis of a least-cost criterion. New capacity (either an additional plant or an expansion of an existing plant) should be added in any period up to the point where the discounted sum of its quasi-rents equals the purchase price plus the marginal value of a particular plant addition (or quasi-rent arising because the capacity expansion is limited). Thus, if

$$I_{jt} > 0, \qquad \text{then} \sum_{t' \geq t} \sigma^{t'-t} \lambda_{3jt} = \beta_{jt} + \lambda_{4jt}. \tag{2.19}$$

The quasi-rent of a plant in any period can be regarded as that part of the supply price set aside to cover depreciation and interest on capital. This is what Turvey (1969:291) calls amortization. If new capacity is added in any period, and if the maximum capacity addition is not reached, demand price in that period is equal to operating cost plus amortization on the new plant plus transmission and distribution cost. Thus, denoting the new plant capacity by n, if

$$x_{nt} > 0 \qquad y_{int} > 0,$$

$$\text{then } g_{int}(y_{int}) = \alpha_{nt} + \lambda_{3nt} + d_{nit}. \tag{2.20}$$

A plant m should begin to be retired when its operating cost rises above the level of $\alpha_{nt} + \lambda_{3nt}$ (given that transmission and distribution costs are the same). Thus, if

$$\alpha_{mt} > \alpha_{nt} + \lambda_{3nt}, \qquad \text{then } x_{mt} = 0. \tag{2.21}$$

Equation (2.19) can be interpreted to mean that the present value of amortization equals the purchase price of new capacity plus the quasi-rent of the capacity limitation. Consequently, the present value of total profit is zero. The issue to be emphasized is that the amount set aside for amortization varies from period to period, depending on demand and perhaps is equal to zero in some periods. With demand varying, a constant proportion of capacity cost each period should not necessarily be recouped. Rather, price should be set to just fully utilize capacity (conditional upon price not being below marginal production cost), and capacity should be selected so that over the life of the plant, capacity cost is just recouped.

Analysis of the Model

By casting the problem in a spatial dimension as well as the temporal dimension, the way has been open to handling many of the knotty problems concerned with investment in generating capacity, as well as the problems involved with price adjustment and allocation over time, by such things as technological change permitting the cheaper transmission of electrical energy over long distances or particularly efficient plants being located at great distances from the consumer (e.g., geothermal generating plants) become realistic.

The general principles of optimal pricing from this model can be summarized as follows:

1. Set prices by time of day (or seasons of the year) in accordance with the pattern of demand. This means that any consumer in a particular hour be treated the same regardless of how much he or she consumes.
2. Vary prices spatially according to verified transmission costs from the respective generating plants of the supply network.
3. Charge the consumer enough to cover the entire marginal distribution cost. This means that it is totally justifiable to charge residential and industrial consumers different prices because the distribution costs for the two classes vary.[11]
4. Marginal price should be raised to the point where demand and supply just clear the market at the given maximum capacity, should demand be sufficient to utilize total generating capacity.
5. Capital costs are imputed to a consumer only to the extent his or her demand presses on the capacity of a specific plant. Thus, no responsibility for capacity costs are attributible to those consumers whose demand does not press upon capacity. What is included here is the treatment of short-run marginal cost and long-run marginal cost. Specifically, in a period where sufficient capacity exists, price should be set equal to the marginal operating cost (i.e., short-run marginal cost).[12] During periods when capacity expansion is necessary, price not only covers the marginal operating cost, but price is set just high enough to compensate for the marginal cost of increasing capacity. The two marginal costs, operating and capital, constitute the long-run marginal cost.[13] The price changes according to the cost and demand conditions.

Note that, if marginal cost equals average cost (constant returns to scale), then the solution also has the property that total cost is exactly covered by revenues. It is possible, however, that marginal cost pricing may yield a revenue which provides a surplus in relation to accounting cost which is too high (occurring when, say, the regulated utility is subject to a ceiling on earnings) or too low (occurring when, say, the utility has been set a target minimum of earnings). If such a financial constraint is absolute, then price must be set below marginal cost in the first instance and above in the second. In either instance where the constraint is binding a welfare loss will be incurred. Turvey[14] discusses the rationale for such a constraint, including a consideration of the gains in managerial efficiency. Ideally, the imposition of a financial constraint would be at a level to provide the necessary incentives and checks for management without requiring any significant departure from the optimal pricing structure outlined above. Some departure is probably inevitable if the constraint is binding, but it need not be large.

REALITY

In the case of most utilities, it is impractical for the pricing policy to account for spatial differences in demand and production costs for individual units. Thus, it is suggested that the service area of a utility be divided into zones, with every consumer in a zone being treated the same. In general the partition could be made in any fashion where each partition represents a subset of the spatial-temporal plane in which price is constant. The administration of any such scheme runs into difficulty, however, because there are no simple rules to indicate when to switch from one partitioned block to another. Consequently, the division would most likely be accomplished along the lines of a rectangular grid coordinate system. The problem formulation, as before, assumes that demand for electrical energy by consumers in a subset of the spatial-temporal plane is independent of the price charged in any other spatial-temporal subset. Thus, no spatial or temporal shift in demand is possible to take advantage of relative price differences.

As an additional consideration, it is currently not feasible to meter the supply of electrical energy to individual consumers on a constantly changing basis from period to period (e.g., hour to hour). What is feasible, however, is to use a somewhat simpler tariff that would change a basic price for off-peak (normal) demand and impose a surcharge for peak demand.

The mechanics of doing this are described in Wenders and Taylor.[15]

SUMMARY

The major issue addressed in this chapter was the optimal price profile for electrical energy where the demand varies spatially as well as temporally and where there are several spatially separated plants with different operating characteristics available for generation. No simple cost-based solution proved possible. Price is not set equal to marginal operating cost. Rather, the price changes according to the cost and demand conditions.

NOTES AND REFERENCES

1. See, for example, R. Turvey and D. Anderson, *Electricity Economics*, Johns Hopkins University Press, Baltimore, 1978 and I: Pressman, "A Mathematical Formulation of the Peak-Load Pricing Problem." *The Bell Journal of Economics and Management Science 1*(Autumn): 304–326, 1970.
2. R. Turvey, "Peak Load Pricing." *Journal of Political Economy 76:* 101–113, 1968.
3. A second consequence of an upward sloping marginal cost curve is that since new additions to capacity incorporate the latest technology, they will have lower operating costs than most of the existing plants. This is more fully explored in N. D. Uri, *Towards an Efficient Allocation of Electrical Energy*. Lexington, Mass.: D.C. Heath and Company, 1975.
4. C. Cicchetti and J. Jurewitz, "Cost, Regulatory Constraint, Averch-Johnson Bias, Peak-Load and Block Pricing." In C. Cicchetti and J. Jurewitz (ed.), *Studies in Electric Utility Regulation.* Cambridge, Mass.: Ballinger Publishing Company, 1975.
5. It is assumed that two plants in close physical proximity are distinct entities.
6. As a general rule, one would not expect $d_{jit} = 13_{kit}$ for $j \neq k$.
7. Following the suggestion of D. Anderson "Models for Determining Least-Cost Investments in Electricity Supply." *The Bell Journal of Economics and Management Science 3*(Spring): 267–299, 1972, operating cost is distinguished from capital cost to allow for explicit treatment of investment.
8. H. Mohring, "The Peak Load Problem with Increasing Returns and Pricing Constraints." *American Economic Review 60:* 693–705, 1970.
9. Joint Committee on Atomic Energy, *Understanding the "National Energy Dilemma.*" Washington, D.C.: U.S. Government Printing Office, 1973.
10. T. Takayama and G. G. Judge, *Spatial and Temporal Price and Allocation Models*. Amsterdam: North-Holland Publishing Company, 1971.
11. R. Turvey, "Marginal Cost." *The Economic Journal LXXIX:* 282–299, 1969.

12. P. O. Steiner, "Peak Loads and Efficient Pricing." *Quarterly Journal of Economics 71*(November): 585–610, 1957.
13. R. Turvey, *Optimal Pricing and Investment in Electricity Supply.* London: George Allen and Unwin, Ltd., 1968.
14. Ibid.
15. J. T. Wenders and L. D. Taylor, "Time-of-Day and Seasonal Pricing Experiments in the Sale of Electric Power," processed, August 1975.

Chapter III

Optimal Pricing: A Case Study

INTRODUCTION

Development planning is a continuous and sequential process involving mobilization and efficient use of resources. In this context the important aspect of development planning in the electrical energy sector is the formulation of suitable policies to carry out the economic activities of the generation, transmission and distribution, and consumption of electrical energy over time and over space. Thus, the problem posed in this chapter is to use the model developed in Chapter II in a planning context to yield an efficient solution with regard to the generation, consumption, and pricing over space for each time period over the planning horizons. It will be demonstrated that within the confines of the model, opportunities exist for increasing the efficiency of pricing and allocating electrical energy in the United States if a departure from past policy is undertaken.

With a view toward empirically implementing the model of Chapter II, as was noted previously, it is necessary to divide the area under consideration into zones or regions. The delineation used here is the standard nine-region division of the contiguous United States.[1] Further since it is not feasible at the practical level to consider individual consumers and individual plants, some aggregation is required. In the case of consumers, since reliable data exist which can be used to estimate the demand functions [i.e., Eq. (2.1)], three consumer classes will be defined for each region: residential, commercial, and industrial.

Each of the sectors exhibits a distinguishable demand for electrical energy. There is a fourth sector, nominally called *other,* consisting of transportation use, government use, agriculture use, railroad use, and interdepartmental use that, across regions, in 1978 accounted for about 4.2 percent of total electrical energy consumed. Because of its small proportion and heterogeneous composition, and because of its overall unresponsiveness to price changes, consideration of the other sector will be pushed into the background where it will be assumed that it can purchase all it desires at the prevailing market price. This will tend to slightly understate net social welfare.

On the supply side, plants are aggregated by fuel type. Three alternative plant types are considered: hydroelectric, fossil-fueled steam plants (i.e., coal, oil, natural gas), and nuclear steam generators. A fourth method of generating electrical energy, internal combustion, is not incorporated into the model. In 1978 it accounted for only 0.4 percent of the electrical energy generated in the United States and is extremely inefficient. The principal applications of internal combustion generators include meeting peak loads, standby service, emergency power, and reserve.

The increasing needs for energy which have followed a pattern of approximately doubling every 10 years emphasize the requirement to look at the longer range problems of investment. To this end, the period 1975–1990 will be focused upon at five-year intervals.

MODEL PARAMETER ESTIMATES

To put the model developed into an operational framework, it is necessary to hypothesize linear demand functions. This converts the problem to one of quadratic programming. Solution algorithms for such problems are readily available. Given this assumption and because of various econometric problems, the estimates of the demand curve coefficients are obtained by first estimating the price elasticity and then translating these elasticities into point estimates of the requisite demand functions.[2] To estimate the elasticity, a variable elasticity model is specified for each consuming sector such that the quantity of electrical energy consumed in any region for a given year is a function of the price of electrical energy for that year, the per capita personal income of that region for that year, and the price of gas in the preceeding year. Upon pooling cross-sectional and time-series data for each consuming sector across all nine regions and for a time period of 1947 to 1978, the price elasticity estimates for 1978 regionally range between −.22 and −.20 for the residential sector, between −.26 and −.31 for the commercial sector, and between −.37 and −.07 for the industrial sector.

Given the temporal nature of the problem, it is necessary to forecast future demand over the horizon. This is accomplished by using the coefficients on the demand model specified, the likely changes in per capita income, the likely changes in the price of electrical energy, and the likely changes in the price of gas. With expected price and expected quantity demanded available, a linear approximation of the demand function for each region, consuming sector and time period is obtained.

On the cost side, marginal interregional transmission cost per kilowatt-hour (kWh) per mile is computed from data suplied by the Federal Power Commission (FPC).[3] The marginal cost of transmitting 1 kWh a distance of 1 mile is 0.004 mills. According to the FPC, this figure is time invariant. Nine demand points are used for the purpose of measuring the distance between regions. (Distance times the marginal cost of transmission will give the cost of transmitting 1 kWh between regions.) The demand areas are fairly large. To select a single representative point in each region, each coordinate in a region is weighted by the consumption of electrical energy at that point, the average distance traveled by each kilowatt-hour, and the maximum distance that electrical energy would have to travel between regions.

Present and projected intraregional distribution cost is obtained directly from the *1970 National Power Survey*[4] (appropriately inflated) and represents an average for electric utilities in the United States. This average can be accepted as a close approximation to the regional distribution cost considering the low level of spatial resolution. The average distribution cost which is expected to remain relatively constant over the time interval will be around 1 cent/kWh. The sum of the transmission and distribution costs yield total delivery cost within and between regions.

The data on the marginal cost of operating a plant (operation and maintenance costs including fuel cost) cannot be regionally disaggregated; so it is necessary to assume identical costs prevail for each plant type across regions. To project what is actually the variable cost component of the total cost in supplying electrical energy, a constant elasticity model is specified where variable cost is a function of net generation. For fossil-fueled steam-electric generation variable cost is also assumed to be a function of thermal efficiency. Using the likely changes in net generation over the horizon, the likely changes in thermal efficiency (for fossil plants), and the coefficients on the cost functions, forecasts for the marginal cost of operating a plant are obtained. The results anticipate, with rising fuel costs, a continued rise in operating costs.

Capital cost, the fixed cost component of the total cost of supplying electrical energy, is estimated using a series of programs developed at Oak Ridge National Laboratory. Based on the assumption that any central station power plant of the same type involves approximately the same major cost components regardless of location or date of initial operation, the programs establish trends in these cost components as a function of time, location, and plant type to estimate cost for a particular case of interest.[5]

Estimates of the limitations on investment in new generating capacity were obtained from the *1970 National Power Survey*.[6] These estimates are looked at here as the most likely additions to capacity. The rate of capital depreciation for each plant type was obtained from a survey of annual reports for companies accounting for virtually all investment and revenue in the privately owned sector of the electrical energy industry.

The choice of the social rate of discount is difficult. From condition (2.15) it is seen that the rate selected will affect the amortization rate of new generating capacity. Considerable literature on selecting the appropriate rate exists. The interested reader is referred to Baumol.[7] While many values are justifiable, a rate of 10 percent, as suggested by Baumol, is adopted.

Two final comments are needed before turning to a solution

of the model. (1) All of the values of the primal variables are in net terms. So, for example, to obtain values for total generation, it would be necessary to inflate the net generation figures by the amount lost upon transmission. (2) All of the values are in 1975 constant dollars.

MODEL SOLUTION

If it is assumed that the maximization of net social welfare is the objective and that a competitive market exists across all plants, consumers, regions, and time periods, and using the data that have been discussed, the solution to the problem of Chapter II can be obtained. Since there is a sizable quantity of data, not all of the results are presented. Only the optimal quantities demanded (Table III.1), prices (Table III.2), gen-

Table III.1. Optimal Demand for Electrical Energy by Sector and Region (in Billions of kWh)

Region	*Year*	*Residential Sector*	*Commercial Sector*	*Industrial Sector*
(1) New England	1975	32.51	24.88	26.85
	1990	71.87	22.79	35.46
(2) Middle Atlantic	1975	92.95	65.20	96.43
	1990	210.34	54.24	120.68
(3) East North Central	1975	118.25	77.23	143.23
	1990	259.10	68.26	194.90
(4) West North Central	1975	56.05	35.61	39.59
	1990	127.32	31.97	51.02
(5) South Atlantic	1975	127.11	75.94	99.16
	1990	285.84	63.77	144.62
(6) East South Central	1975	58.76	18.63	94.87
	1990	111.24	13.88	158.86
(7) West South Central	1975	77.43	59.89	81.87
	1990	172.85	50.50	124.98
(8) Mountain	1975	25.33	23.48	26.25
	1990	54.49	18.63	37.66
(9) Pacific	1975	94.27	73.94	83.53
	1990	203.97	54.76	116.34

Table III.2. Optimal Demand Price by Region in Cents per kWh[a,b]

Region	*1975*	*1990*
(1) New England	3.34	4.77
	(4.10)	
(2) Middle Atlantic	3.28	4.29
	(3.93)	2.93
(3) East North Central	2.34	2.93
	(2.72)	
(4) West North Central	2.36	3.02
	(2.65)	
(5) South Atlantic	2.65	3.69
	(2.94)	
(6) East South Central	1.83	3.01
	(1.93)	
(7) West South Central	1.96	4.77
	(2.10)	
(8) Mountain	2.01	3.96
	(2.23)	
(9) Pacific	1.98	3.92
	(2.07)	

Notes: (a) In constant 1975 dollars
(b) Actual 1975 prices in parentheses

eration (Tables III.3 and III.4), capacity additions (Table III.5), and the quasi-rent (Table III.6) are given for the beginning and ending years (1975 and 1990, respectively).

There are significant interregional transmissions of electrical energy that would have been desirable from the net social welfare maximization criterion in 1975. (Interregional transmission is not yet a normal part of the electrical energy picture.) Because of the better alignment of capacity costs over time, the quantity of the interregional flows falls to zero by 1990.

The optimal quantities demanded by each sector for each of the regions changes from the amount actually consumed in 1975 as one would expect given that a uniform price is charged to each of the consuming sectors. The optimal quantity demanded by the residential sector increases about 5 percent in

Table III.3. Optimal Flows of Electrical Energy Generated in 1975 by Region (in Billions of kWh)

From To	*NE*[1]	*MA*	*ENC*	*WNC*	*SA*	*ESC*	*WSC*	*M*	*P*
(1) NE	84.23	6.55							
(2) MA		248.02							
(3) ENC			310.12						
(4) WNC			28.58	131.25					
(5) SA					262.01				
(6) ESC					40.19	172.26			
(7) WSC							219.19		
(8) M								75.06	
(9) P									251.74

Note: 1. NE denotes the New England region, MA denotes the Middle Atlantic region, and so forth.

Table III.4. Optimal Flows of Electrical Energy Generated in 1990 by Region (in Billions of kWh)

From To	*NE*	*MA*	*ENC*	*WNC*	*SA*	*ESC*	*WSC*	*M*	*P*
(1) NE	130.12								
(2) MA		385.26							
(3) ENC			522.26						
(4) WNC				210.31					
(5) SA					494.24				
(6) ESC						283.98			
(7) WSC							348.33		
(8) M								110.78	
(9) P									375.06

Table III.5. Optimal Investment in New Generating Capacity by Region (in Billions of kWh)

Region	*Year*	*Hydroelectric Plants*	*Fossil Plants*	*Nuclear Plants*
(1) New England	1990	2.41	0.0	36.55
(2) Middle Atlantic	1990	21.46	0.0	88.75
(3) East North Central	1990	19.55	5.56	118.26
(4) West North Central	1990	3.70	0.0	61.20
(5) South Atlantic	1990	9.84	80.90	78.84
(6) East South Central	1990	14.52	0.0	46.14
(7) West South Central	1990	0.0	0.0	102.22
(8) Mountain	1990	8.93	0.0	18.93
(9) Pacific	1990	45.48	0.0	44.80

Table III.6. Quasi-rent of a Plant by Region (in 0.1 Cents per kWh)

Region	*Year*	*Hydroelectric Plants*	*Fossil Plants*	*Nuclear Plants*
(1) New England	1975	8.69	0.0	1.03
	1990	2.20	0.0	0.0
(2) Middle Atlantic	1975	10.34	0.72	1.87
	1990	3.00	0.0	0.0
(3) East North Central	1975	13.90	4.64	5.36
	1990	3.07	0.0	0.37
(4) West North Central	1975	8.65	0.0	1.37
	1990	1.76	0.0	0.0
(5) South Atlantic	1975	9.48	1.67	2.46
	1990	1.51	0.0	0.27
(6) East South Central	1975	8.38	0.0	0.88
	1990	2.23	0.0	0.0
(7) West South Central	1975	6.91	0.0	1.29
	1990	0.0	0.0	0.0
(8) Mountain	1975	9.79	0.71	2.23
	1990	2.23	0.0	0.0
(9) Pacific	1975	8.40	0.0	0.0
	1990	3.02	0.0	0.0

each of the regions over the actual 1975 value, and the optimal quantity demanded by the commercial sector increases by about 15 percent. For the industrial sector, the optimal quantity demanded falls about 14 percent from the actual 1975 value. Thus, in 1975 not only were the residential and commercial sectors on the average charged too high a price for the electrical energy they consumed, they also were allocated less than the amount the societal optimum would dictate.

The marginal-cost pricing concept is at work in the model to determine the optimal pricing scheme. When capacity is fully utilized, the full marginal cost consisting of the variable cost, delivery cost, and investment cost is charged. In an off-peak period when no new capacity needs to be added, the charge is limited to the marginal operating cost and delivery cost.

The overall price profile that results is a most revealing aspect of the model. If one truly believes that the electrical energy industry should be regulated in such a way as to maximize net social welfare, then the regulatory commissions are sadly remiss in setting the rate structure. As noted above, not only should a uniform price be charged to each sector for the homogeneous good, which currently is not the practice, but this price will follow a trajectory of increasing slightly through 1990. Ignoring the price differentials among sectors in a given region, the average price paid for electrical energy in 1975 (see Table III.2) given the existing capacity constraints is in the neighborhood of 5 to 20 percent too high. This inefficiency will continue in subsequent periods and become more pronounced if the projected trend in prices occurs. Using average prices again across a region, the price that is expected to be charged will be in the range of twice what the competitive solution suggests is optimal.

As noted previously, costs are the most significant consideration in the economic analysis of determining the least-cost investment in electrical energy generation. Capacity expansion (investment) decisions in any period depend upon the future evolution of factor prices. The optimal condition of Chapter II indicates that when capacity is added, investment in the plant with the lowest combined operating cost, delivery cost, and capital cost is undertaken first up to the permissible limit. Subsequently, capacity is added to the plant with the second lowest combined cost while imposing a penalty on society because capacity of the first plant is limited. This process is repeated until consumers are supplied with the amount of electrical energy for which they are willing to pay.

Note that with only a few exceptions across all time periods and regions, hydroelectric additions are undertaken first with nuclear plants second. The fossil additions to capacity make up the residual supply, falling to zero in some regions in the later period. In the first period in which investment is permitted (i.e., 1980), the additions to capacity for each plant in almost all regions are undertaken to the maximum limit. However, as the year 1990 is approached, investment activity falls away from the limit in most instances except for hydroelectric plants. In fact in 1990, the optimal solution indicates that minimal investment in fossil plants should occur. If this is the pattern that develops, the electrical energy industry must continually revise its investment plans and limit actual investment in new nuclear and fossil generating facilities accordingly.

Focusing on the year 1975, observe the quasi-rent (marginal value) of the various plants (Table III.6). This quasi-rent ranges as high as 1.39 cents/kWh and as low as zero. This says that if generating capacity had been expanded by 1 kWh, net social welfare would have increased between 0 and 1.39 cents, depending on the plant and region in which the expansion occurred. Of course, the development of generating capacity depends on a myriad of factors, any of which limit the expansion of existing capacity. Nevertheless, it is instructive to see what benefit would accrue if additional capacity had been available. If expected additions to new capacity materialize, this marginal value will fall dramatically toward zero for fossil and nuclear plants and become increasingly smaller for hydroelectric plants. This result indicates that a concerted effort be made in expanding hydroelectric sites beyond the physical and technological limitations existing as long as the operating cost, delivery costs and capital cost do not exceed those of the other plants. If it is true that only 30 percent of the total potential capacity of hydroelectric plants has been developed,[8] it would serve society well to invest in the research and development efforts required to expand hydroelectric capacity beyond the anticipated limitations. Alternately, other generating methods (e.g., geothermal and solar) might be investigated more intensely if it is expected that capital costs can be made to compare favorably with the more traditional plant types. If only modest increases in expenditures are needed for undertaking fruitful research and development, then such increased expenditure is justified conditional upon the benefit (a reduction in the marginal value of a plant type) ouweighing the cost.

SUMMARY

This chapter set out to apply the model of Chapter II in a context that would aid in formulating suitable policies to carry out the economic activities of generating, transmitting and distributing, and consuming electrical energy over time and over space. Within its confines, it has been shown what the investment profile for new generating capacity as well as the price and allocation of electrical energy should resemble over the period 1975–1990 for the United States.

NOTES AND REFERENCES

1. The regional classification is as follows: (1) New England (Maine, New Hampshire, Vermont, Massachusetts, Rhode Island, Connecticut), (2) Middle Atlantic (New York, New Jersey, Pennsylvania), (3) East North Central (Ohio, Indiana, Illinois, Michigan, Wisconsin), (4) West North Central (Minnesota, Iowa, Missouri, North Dakota, South Dakota, Nebraska, Kansas), (5) South Atlantic (Delaware, Maryland and Washington, D.C., Virginia, West Virginia, North Carolina, Georgia, Florida), (6) East South Central (Kentucky, Tennessee, Alabama, Mississippi), (7) West South Central, (Arkansas, Louisana, Oklahoma, Texas), (8) Mountain (Montana, Idaho, Wyoming, Colorado, New Mexico, Arizona, Utah, Nevada), and (9) Pacific (Washington, Oregon, California).
2. N. D. Uri, *Towards an Efficient Allocation of Electrical Energy,* Lexington, Mass.: D.C. Heath and Company, 1975, contains the mechanics of doing this.
3. Federal Power Commission, *The 1970 National Power Survey.* Washington, D.C.: U.S. Government Printing Office, 1971.
4. Ibid.
5. H. I. Bowers, *CONCEPT—Computerized Conceptual Cost Estimates of Steam—Electric Power Plants,* Oak Ridge, Tenn.: Oak Ridge National Laboratory, 1977.
6. Federal Power Commission, Op. Cit.
7. W. J. Baumol, "On the Social Rate of Discount." *American Economic Review 58*(September): 785–802, 1968.
8. Federal Power Commission, *Hydroelectric Power Resources of the United States, Developed and Undeveloped.* Washington, D.C.: U.S. Government Printing Office, 1972.

Chapter IV

Pricing Public Utility Service when Profit Is Subject to Regulatory Constraint

INTRODUCTION

In this chapter a model is developed combining spatial variation with the temporal element of electrical energy demand and supply to determine the optimal pricing scheme for a public utility whose profit is regulated.

The optimal capacity of the plant and the pricing of the utility services are dependent on the set of assumptions used to define the problem. Turvey[1] examines the most important of these assumptions and discusses the implications of removing them for electrical energy tariffs. One of these (the one relevant here) rests on the empirical observation that an electric utility production technique consists of employing plants that have different cost characteristics according to their role in meeting demand. The assumption of constant marginal operating cost and constant incremental capacity cost is too simple to be meaningful. He notes that for an electrical energy system consisting of plants of different vintage, location, and type and consequently operating cost, the system marginal-operating-cost curve is upward sloping. What is important then is the determination of the relevant pricing decisions when it is possible to employ more than one plant to meet demand.

The solution to the problem of determining optimal prices for public utility service where demand varies over space and over time is based on a model developed by Samuelson[2] and refined by Takayama and Judge[3] and Takayama and Woodland.[4] The general model is adapted to accomodate the peculiarities of the market for electrical energy.

FRAMEWORK OF THE ANALYSIS

Visualize an economy where there are many consumers of electrical energy and many generating plants each of which are spatially separated. To formulate the understanding and development of the model, the following definitions and notation are introduced:

Let $i = 1, 2, ..., N$ denote the consumers;
$j = 1, 2, ..., \theta$ denote the generating plants;[5]
$t, \tau = 1, 2, ..., T$ denote the discrete time periods of equal length;
y_{ijt} = quantity of electrical energy demanded by consumer i from plant j in period t;
x_{jit} = quantity of electrical energy supplied by plant j to consumer i in period t;
x_{jt} = quantity of electrical energy generated by plant j in period t;
I_{jt} = investment in new capacity for plant j that will be available for operation in period t;
I_{jt} = maximum possible investment in new capacity for plant j in period t;
K_{j1} = generating capacity of plant j in period 1;
d_{jit} = delivery cost (including transmission and distribution costs) by plant j to consumer i in period t;[6]
β_{jt} = cost of capital for an additional unit of generating capacity for plant j in period t;
α_{jt} = operating cost (including fuel cost) for plant j in period t;
r = rate of interest.

Relying on an assumption that the demand functions of each consumer for each time period are known with certainty or are available in the certainty equivalence sense, the demand functions are given in the form

$$P_{ijt} = g_{ijt}(y_{ijt}), \tag{4.1}$$

where P_{ijt} is the price of electrical energy to consumer i from plant j in period t. The implications of this assumption are discussed by Mohring.[7]

The search for optimum demands, prices, and operating schedules is subject to a number of constraints:

1. For each plant in each time period, the total quantity of electrical energy generated by a plant must be greater than or equal to the quantity demanded by all consumers from that plant:

$$y_{jt} \leq \sum_{i} x_{jit}, \tag{4.2}$$

where the total quantity of electrical energy demanded from plant j is the sum of the quantities demanded by all consumers:

$$y_{jt} = \sum_{i} y_{ijt}. \tag{4.3}$$

2. For each plant and each time period, the total generation of electrical energy is greater than or equal to the quantity supplied by that plant to all consumers:

$$\sum_{i} x_{jit} \leq x_{jt}. \tag{4.4}$$

3. For each plant and each time period, total generation is less than or equal to the generation from that plant existing in the initial period plus the generation from new capacity added in the first and subsequent periods:

$$x_{jt} \leq K_{j1} + \sum_{\tau=1}^{t} I_{j\tau}. \tag{4.5}$$

There is a temptation to include a term to account for the rate of decline in output over time due to "age." However, since it is not significant for well-maintained generating plants, the term is excluded. Further, if capacity is not added in period t or the plant does not exist in the initial period, I_{jt} or K_{j1} will be appropriately zero.

4. For each region, investment in generating capacity of a plant is constrained by physical, institutional, and technological limitations:

$$I_{jt} \leq \hat{I}_{jt}. \tag{4.6}$$

For example, it is well recognized that there is a maximum feasible expansion in, say, nuclear power development considering the constraints imposed by such things as licensing, development of additional uranium supplies, technical and construction manpower limitations, difficulties with new and extrapolated equipment, and so on.[8]

5. For each plant, consumer, and time period there is a maximum transmission of electrical energy:

$$x_{jit} \leq \hat{x}_{jit}, \tag{4.7}$$

where $\hat{x}_{jit}$ is the maximum and technologically feasible interregional transmission.

Before proceeding, a number of points need to be clarified concerning the economic environment:

1. Additions to capacity are looked upon as an average. To include a margin of spare capacity required to meet demands above the mean expectation; the I_{jt} can be inflated by the appropriate margin.
2. There is no discussion of terminal conditions. This does not preclude such discussions in a variant of the model.
3. The formulation is deterministic. Accounting for uncertainties in demand, plant availability, and so forth can be included in the margin of spare capacity factor.

A MODEL FOR PROFIT MAXIMIZATION

Assume the public utility (hereafter, the firm) has as its objective the maximization of profit and is not subject to regulatory constraint. The problem may be stated as follows. Maximize profit Π:

$$\Pi = \underset{t}{\pi}\, \sigma^{t-1} \left\{ \left[\sum_i \sum_j g_{ijt}(y_{ijt}) y_{ijt} - \sum_j \alpha_{jt} x_{jt} - \sum_j \beta_{jt} I_{jt} \right.\right.$$
$$\left.\left. - \sum_i \sum_j d_{jit} x_{jit} \right] \right\}, \tag{4.8}$$

where $\sigma^{t-1} = 1/(1 + r)^{t-1}$.

Providing the demand functions are downward sloping, the

objective function is concave and the Kuhn–Tucker conditions will give the necessary and sufficient conditions for a competitive solution.[9]

Associate the dual variables $\sigma^{t-1}\rho_{1jt}$, $\sigma^{t-1}\rho_{2jt}$, $\sigma^{t-1}\rho_{3jt}$, $\sigma^{t-1}\rho_{4jt}$, and $\sigma^{t-1}\rho_{5jit}$ with constraints (4.2) and (4.4) through (4.7). Multiplying through by σ^{t-1} where appropriate, the Kuhn-Tucker conditions are

$$y_{jt} \leq \sum_i x_{jit} \qquad \rho_{1jt} \geq 0 \tag{4.9}$$

$$\sum_j x_{jit} \leq x_{jt} \qquad \rho_{2jt} \geq 0 \tag{4.10}$$

$$x_{jt} \leq K_{j1} + \sum_{\tau=1}^{t} I_{j\tau} \qquad \rho_{3jt} \geq 0 \tag{4.11}$$

$$I_{jt} \leq \hat{I}_{jt} \qquad \rho_{4jt} \geq 0 \tag{4.12}$$

$$x_{jit} \leq \hat{x}_{jit} \qquad \rho_{5jit} \geq 0 \tag{4.13}$$

$$y_{ijt}g'_{ijt}(y_{ijt}) + g_{ijt}(y_{ijt}) \leq \rho_{1jt} \qquad y_{ijt} \geq 0 \tag{4.14}$$

$$\rho_{1jt} \leq d_{jit} + \rho_{2jt} + \rho_{5jit} \qquad x_{jit} \geq 0 \tag{4.15}$$

$$\rho_{2jt} \leq \alpha_{jt} + \rho_{3jt} \qquad x_{jt} \geq 0 \tag{4.16}$$

$$\sum_{t' \geq t} \sigma^{t'-t}\rho_{3jt'} \leq \beta_{jt} + \rho_{4jt} \qquad I_{jt} \geq 0 \tag{4.17}$$

ρ_{3jt} can be interpreted as the quasi-rent of plant j in period t and, if that plant is utilized, is equal to the total marginal cost minus marginal operating cost. Thus, if

$$x_{jt} > 0, \qquad \text{then } \rho_{3jt} = \rho_{2jt} - \alpha_{jt}. \tag{4.18}$$

Suppose, in addition, $y_{ijt} > 0$ and $0 < x_{jit} < \hat{x}_{jit}$. To minimize total cost, production will be scheduled on equipment in increasing order of operating cost and delivery cost. Therefore, the marginal revenue[10] from a consumer in period t equals the distribution and transmission costs plus operating cost on the least-efficient plant, denoted by j*, being used to generate electrical energy. Thus, if

$$0 < x_{j^*t} < K_{j^*t} + \sum_{\tau=1}^{t} I_{j^*t}, \qquad \text{then } MR_{ij^*t} = \alpha_{j^*t} + d_{j^*it}. \tag{4.19}$$

The quasi-rent of any plant ρ_{3jt} in use is equal to the difference between its operating cost plus distribution cost plus transmission cost and these costs accounted for by the least-efficient plant. Thus, if

$$x_{jt} > 0, \qquad \text{then } \rho_{3jt} = \alpha_{j^*t} + d_{j^*it} - (\alpha_{jt} + d_{jit} + \rho_{5jit}). \qquad (4.20)$$

Observe that it is possible to use a plant to generate electrical energy that does not have the lowest operating cost. If the delivery cost is sufficiently large or there is a constraint on transmission, then it would be optimal to use a plant with a higher operating cost while shutting down a more efficient one.

Additions to capacity are undertaken on the basis of a least-cost criterion. New capacity (either an additional plant or an expansion of an existing plant) should be added in any period up to the plant where the discounted sum of its quasi-rents equals the purchase price plus the marginal value of a particular plant addition (or quasi-rent arising because the capacity expansion is limited). Thus, if

$$I_{jt} > 0, \qquad \text{then } \sum_{t' \geq t} \sigma^{t'-t} \rho_{3jt'} = \beta_{jt} + \rho_{4jt}. \qquad (4.21)$$

The quasi-rent of a plant in any period can be regarded as that part of the supply price set aside to cover depreciation and interest on capital. This is what Turvey calls *amortization.*[11] If new capacity is added in any period, and if the maximum capacity addition is not reached, demand price in that period is equal to operating cost plus amortization on the new plant plus transmission and distribution cost. Thus, denoting the new plant capacity by n, if

$$x_{nt} > 0, \qquad y_{int} > 0, \qquad x_{int} < \hat{x}_{int},$$

$$\text{then } MR_{int} = \alpha_{nt} + \rho_{3nt} + d_{nit}. \qquad (4.22)$$

A plant m should begin to be retired when its operating cost rises above the level of $\alpha_{nt} + \rho_{3nt}$ (given the transmission and distributing costs and transmission restrictions are the same). Thus, if

$$\alpha_{mt} > \alpha_{nt} + \beta_{nt}, \qquad \text{then} \quad x_{mt} = 0. \qquad (4.23)$$

Equation (4.21) can be interpreted to mean that the present

value of amortization equals the purchase price of new capacity plus the quasi-rent of the capacity limitation. The issue to be emphasized is that the amount set aside for amortization varies from period to period.

Analysis of the Model

The general principles of optimal pricing when the firm is allowed to operate as an unregulated monopolist can be summarized as follows:

1. Set prices by time of day (or seasons of the year) in accordance with the pattern of demand. This means that the marginal revenue from any consumer in a particular hour be the same as any other consumer.
2. Vary prices spatially depending upon how far the consumer is from the generating plant(s) and what their demand elasticity is. Thus, it is possible that a consumer farther from a particular generating plant but with a larger price elasticity of demand will be paying the same or may be even a lower price then a consumer closer to the generating plant if this latter consumer's price elasticity is smaller.
3. Charge the consumer on the basis of total marginal cost. This means that if a residential and industrial consumer were identical in all respects (e.g., demand elasticities, distance from the generating plant) it would be justifiable to charge the residential consumer a higher price because the distribution cost for the two classes are different.[12]
4. Capital costs are imputed to a consumer only to the extent his or her demand presses on the capacity of a specific plant. Thus, any increase in demand during peak periods requiring a utility to expand its generating capacity will result in a charge to a consumer to compensate for the increased cost associated with satisfying that consumer's demand.

PROFIT MAXIMIZATION SUBJECT TO REGULATORY CONSTRAINT

Now introduce a regulatory limit which holds profit at or below some level which will generally increase as the size of the system is increased. Three particular forms for the profit ceiling will be considered.

The first method of regulation limits the firm's profits to a fixed amount per unit of output. Thus a utility has its profit equal to some fraction of a cent per kilowatt-hour γ such that

$$\pi_{1jt} \leq \gamma x_{jt}, \tag{4.24}$$

where π_{1jt} is the profit on the net generation by plant j in period t.

Combining this regulatory constraint with the profit-maximization objective means maximizing Eq. (4.8) subject to constraints (4.2), (4.4) through (4.7), and (4.24).

Making the same assumptions with regard to the demand functions and associating the dual variables as before and associating the dual variable $\sigma^{t-1}\rho_{6jt}$ with constraint (4.24), the Kuhn–Tucker conditions can be obtained. All of them will be the same with the exception of Eq. (4.16), which becomes

$$\rho_{2jt} \leq \alpha_{jt} + \rho_{3jt} - \rho_{6jt}\gamma \qquad x_{jt} \geq 0, \tag{4.16a}$$

and the addition of

$$\pi_{1jt} \leq \gamma x_{jt} \qquad \rho_{6jt} \geq 0 \tag{4.25}$$

Condition (4.16a) is the one with significant regulatory implications. When the quantity of electrical energy generated by a particular plant is positive, then the marginal cost will equal the marginal operating cost plus quasi-rent less the marginal profitability of an additional unit of output. Since this latter term is (in all probability) positive, the marginal cost will not be any higher than in the unregulated case and in all likelihood will be lower. Hence, given a positive demand on this plant, a lower marginal revenue from each consumer is implied, and with a downward-sloping demand curve, this means a larger output with a lower price. Thus, under regulation limiting profit per unit of output, any unit of output will result in a lower marginal revenue than in the unregulated case. All consumers benefit equally. Finally, because the return is applied uniformly to every unit of output, the sequence in which generating units are brought into service (i.e., by the least-cost criterion) will not be altered from the profit-maximization situation.

A second method of regulation permits the firm to obtain a fair return on total costs. Denoting the fair return by μ, then

$$\pi_{2t} \leq \mu \left(\sum_j \alpha_{jt} x_{jt} - \sum_j \beta_{jt} I_{jt} - \sum_i \sum_j d_{jit} x_{jit} - \sum_i \sum_j f_{jit} x_{jit} \right), \quad (4.26)$$

where π_{2t} is the profit on total costs in period t.

It is a straightforward matter to associate the dual variable $\sigma^{t-1}\rho_{7t}$ with this constraint and proceed as before. Going through the mathematics of the argument, it can be shown that regulation utilizing a fair-return-on-total-cost criterion will reduce marginal revenues by the same amount for all plants and all time periods. The result will be analogous to that observed with the previous criterion.

A third method of regulation, and the one most widely used, utilizes a return-on-investment criterion. Under this method the firm's earnings may not exceed a fixed amount, μ, for each unit of installed capacity:

$$\pi_{3jt} \leq \mu \left(K_{j1} + \sum_{\tau=1}^{t} I_{j\tau} \right). \quad (4.27)$$

Assuming that profit maximization is the objective and that constraint (4.27) is added to constraints (4.2) and (4.4) through (4.7), the optimality conditions can be derived. For downward-sloping demand functions and the dual variables defined as before and for dual variable $\sigma^{t-1}\rho_{8jt}$ associated with constraint (4.27), the Kuhn–Tucker conditions are the same as before with the exception of (4.17), which becomes

$$\sum_{t' \geq t} \sigma^{t-t'} \rho_{3jt'} \leq \beta_{jt} + \rho_{4jt} - \mu \sum_{t' \geq t} \sigma^{t'-t} \rho_{8jt'}, \quad (4.17a)$$

and the addition of

$$\pi_{3jt} = \mu \left(K_{j1} + \sum_{\tau=1}^{t} I_{j\tau} \right) \qquad \rho_{8jt} \geq 0. \quad (4.28)$$

This says as before that additions to capacity are undertaken on the basis of a least-cost criterion. Now, however new capacity should be added in any period up to the point where the discounted sum of its quasi-rents equals the purchase price plus the marginal value of a particular plant addition minus the discounted sum of the marginal profitability of a particular plant addition. This latter term can be regarded as that part of the supply price set aside to provide a fair rate of return on investment for each unit of generating capacity.

In this case regulation will result in a lowering of the price to each consumer from the monopoly level so long as capacity expansion is positive. This will happen because the quasi-rent of a plant will be lower in any period (lower by the marginal profitability). With a lower quasi-rent, total marginal cost will be adjusted downward. Equating marginal revenue for each consumer to this lower marginal cost results in a larger output at a lower price. Thus, the regulator achieves the goal that output is increased from the monopoly level. It is possible that the adjusted marginal cost will be sufficiently lower so that capacity will be larger than the level required were price equated to actual marginal cost. One is observing with this method of regulation the Averch–Johnson effect.[13] There will be an overbuilding of capacity because profits increase with the level of capacity. The firm will pass along the benefits of regulation to those consumers whose increased demand causes an increase in capacity.

The expansion of capacity and the size of the fair rate of return μ are related in a predictable way. Namely, the closer the fair rate is to the cost of capital, the larger will be the capacity. This can be seen by observing that the lower the quasi-rent of a plant is, the closer is the cost of capital to the rate of return and thus, by condition (4.21), the larger will be the capacity.

Implications of the Regulatory Constraints

Before discussing the implications of the pricing of electrical energy under the different regulatory practices, a summary of the results is presented.

The method of regulation limiting the firm's profits to a fixed amount per unit output equates marginal revenues to something less than marginal costs for all consumers. Any unit of output regardless of to whom it is sold, regardless of when it is generated and regardless of the plant on which it is generated will bring a lower marginal revenue than in the unregulated monopoly case.

Permitting a fair return on total costs involves a proportional lowering of marginal revenues in all periods disregarding consumer and plant identities.

The firm constrained to earn at most a fair return on its capital investment will set rates below the monopoly level in periods when new capacity is added and at the monopoly level when no new capacity is needed.

A comparison of the various methods of regulation when consumers and producers are spatially diffuse shows that the method of regulation can have a substantial effect on the distribution of price reductions between consumers inducing an expansion in capacity (peak consumers) and those utilizing only existing capacity (off-peak consumers). Under rate-of-return regulation, the reductions in the price are received entirely by the peak period consumers. Capacity is expanded from the profit-maximizing level toward (and perhaps even past) the economically optimal (price equal to marginal cost) level. This method of regulation thus provides an advantage in that it dampens the monopolistic tendency to restrict output, but it also entails the disadvantage that off-peak consumers do not share in the price reductions. This latter problem is corrected by the alternative methods of constraint. Under regulations limiting profit per unit of output, all consumers share in price reductions regardless of whether they utilize peak or off-peak service. The rule for regulation limiting return on costs is that the same percentage decrease in marginal revenue be given in peak or in off-peak periods. Under all three constraints, regulation is effective in that monopoly profits are reduced from the unregulated level and generating capacity is larger.

The spatial implications for pricing electrical energy are an obvious extension of the general principles of optimal pricing presented above. Prices will be varied depending on how far the consumer is from the generating plant. Regulation will have the effect of lowering prices.

SUMMARY

The principal question addressed in this chapter was the optimal price profile for a regulated public utility where the demand varies spatially as well as temporally and where there are several spatially separated plants with different operating characteristics available for generation. No simple cost based solution proved possible. Under regulatory constraint, regardless of its form, price will be reduced as the output of the public utility is expanded. The method of regulation does make a difference in the distribution of price reductions between consumers. Under a system where profit is limited to a fixed amount per unit output and a system where profit is limited to a fair return on total costs, prices will be proportionally lower for all consumers regardless of location and the time period in which they consume electrical energy. The firm constrained to earn a fair return on its capital investment, however, will set prices to favor the consumers, causing an expansion in generating capacity.

NOTES AND REFERENCES

1. R. Turvey, "Peak Load Pricing." *Journal of Political Economy 76:* 101–113, 1968.
2. P. A. Samuelson, "Spatial Price Equilibrium and Linear Programming." *The American Economic Review 42*(June): 283–303, 1952.
3. T. Takayama and G. G. Judge, "Equilibrium Among Spatially Separated Markets: A Reformulation." *Econometrica 32*(October): 510–524, 1964.
4. T. Takayama and A. D. Woodland, "Equivalence of Price and Quantity Formulations of Spatial Equilibrium: Purified Duality in Quadratic and Concave Programming." *Econometrica 38*(November): 889:;906, 1970.
5. It is assumed that two plants in close physical proximity are distinct entities.
6. As a general rule one would not expect the delivery cost to two distinct individuals from a given plant to be identical since, for example, it is more expensive to distribute electrical energy to residential consumers than to industrial consumers. See Foster Associates, Inc., *Energy Prices 1960–1973,* Cambridge, Mass.: Ballinger Publishing Company, 1974.
7. Mohring argues that for the demand price of a commodity to depend only on its output level requires that a utility function can be written in an additive form dependent on the inverse demand function. See H. Mohring, "The Peak Load Problem with Increasing Returns and Pricing Constraints," *The American Economic Review 60:* 693–705, 1960.
8. Joint Committee on Atomic Energy, *Understanding the National Energy Dilemma.* Washington, D.C.: U.S. Government Printing Office, 1973.
9. T. Takayama and G. G. Judge, *Spatial and Temporal Price and Allocation Models.* Amsterdam: North-Holland Publishing Company, 1971.
10. $[d\ g_{ijt}(y_{ijt})/dy_{ijt}]y_{ijt} = MR_{ijt}$, where MR denotes marginal revenue.
11. R. Turvey, "Marginal Cost." *The Economic Journal LXXIX:* 282–299, 1969.
12. Foster Associates, Inc., Ibid.
13. H. Averch and L. Johnson, "Behavior of the Firm Under Regulatory Constraint." *The American Economic Review 5:* 1053–1069, 1962.

Chapter V

Optimal Pricing under Regulation: The Case Study Extended

INTRODUCTION

Following the model developed in the previous chapter, assume that the generation of electrical energy is completely controlled by a central authority whose behavior is that of a monopolist. Additionally, assume that plants of three types exist (hydroelectric, fossil, and nuclear), that there are three identifiable consuming sectors in any location demanding electrical energy (residential, commercial, and industrial), that the monopolist buys its factors of production (labor, fuel, and capital equipment) in competitive markets, and that resale of electrical energy among consuming sectors is not possible. Next assume a regional disaggregation along the lines previously used. Finally assume that, from the empirical point of view, the regional demand and cost functions are the same as those developed in Chapter III.

It is important to emphasize the crucial assumption of no resale among regions, which means that arbitrager's actions in each region are completely suppressed, and thus the central authority can practice price discrimination.[1] Assume that the transmission and distribution activities play passive roles in transmitting and distributing a given quantity determined by the central authority from one region to another at a fixed kilowatthour rate. Within this setting the objective of the central authority is to maximize total profits over all regions and for all time periods where the profit from sales over all of the regions for all of the time periods is that given by Eq. (4.8).

It should be clear that under a pricing-allocation scheme that maximizes profits for the central authority, the market prices between two regions may differ by more than the delivery cost, and consequently the price system of the central authority may be quite different from that achieved under perfect competition.

As before, the demand quantities and supply quantities of electrical energy must satisfy the constraints delineated in the previous chapter.

THE MONOPOLY SOLUTION

The profit-maximization problem can now be solved. The assumptions, again, are that there are no restrictions on interregional flows, there are nine regions (see note 1 of Chapter III), three plants per region, and four time periods.

It is well known that monopoly will lead to a nonoptimal resource allocation. The efficiency conditions for a competitive solution will normally be violated by the monopoly market structure.[2] Note, however, that the only distinction necessarily implied by the pure theory of competition and monopoly is the fact that the monopolist's price exceeds marginal cost, while the price in the perfectly competitive market just equals marginal cost. It is solely on this basis that monopoly leads to an allocation of electrical energy that is inefficient.[3]

Assuming that a monopolistic market controlled by a central authority prevails across all consuming and producing sectors, all regions, and all time periods, the solution to the problem can be found. Once again because of the myriad of numbers, not all of the results are presented. Only the optimal price (Table V.1), generation (Tables V.2 and V.3), capacity additions (Table V.4), and quasi-rents on each plants (Table V.5) are given. The technique used to obtain quantity demanded is discussed below.

The revealing results of this solution are best looked at in comparison with the perfectly competitive solution of Chapter III. It is to be expected that social welfare will be enhanced with the elimination of a central authority whose objective it

Table V.1. Monopoly demand price by region (in cents per kWh)[a]

	Residential Sector		*Commercial Sector*		*Industrial Sector*	
Region	*1975*	*1990*	*1975*	*1990*	*1975*	*1990*
(1) New England	12.19	13.62	7.26	8.36	6.87	7.59
(2) Middle Atlantic	12.73	13.81	7.78	8.59	6.57	7.37
(3) East North Central	10.08	11.99	6.31	7.75	6.67	7.45
(4) West North Central	9.72	10.23	6.01	7.42	6.18	7.29
(5) South Atlantic	8.78	9.05	8.97	10.03	6.82	8.02
(6) East South Central	6.59	8.13	4.67	6.20	15.05	12.31
(7) West South Central	8.53	9.87	4.98	6.63	10.42	11.97
(8) Mountain	8.82	10.06	5.12	7.11	9.21	10.76
(9) Pacific	7.46	8.88	4.84	5.23	20.16	21.71

Note: a. In constant 1975 dollars.

is to maximize profits.[4] The magnitude of this increase can be calculated from the values of the net social welfare. If a central authority were allowed to operate as a monopolist in pricing and allocating electrical energy, the discounted net social welfare would fall by 49.2 percent over the 15-year period from the competitive norm.

In just what form would total welfare decline? First note that the prices paid by each consuming sector in a region are no longer uniform. The values found in Table V.1 are prices for each consuming sector for the region. (To obtain the price paid by a consuming sector, one takes the demand curve that is appropriate and multiply the coefficients by one-half—recall that the demand curves are linear functions. Once this is done, setting the appropriate marginal revenue equal to this linear function will yield the optimal quantity demanded. Substituting this quantity demanded back into the original linear demand function will yield the price paid by the consuming sector.)

With prices radically changing, the quantity demanded departs appreciably from the competitive solution. Using 1975 as the base, the quantity of electrical energy demanded by the resi-

Table V.2. Flows of Electrical Energy Generated in 1975 by Region for the Monopoly Model (in Billions of kWh).

From/To	*NE*[1]	*MA*	*ENC*	*WNC*	*SA*	*ESC*	*WSC*	*M*	*P*
1. NE	42.70								
2. MA		131.06							
3. ENC			179.68						
4. WNC				66.92					
5. SA					154.88				
6. ESC						87.41			
7. WSC							110.26		
8. M								39.11	
9. P									131.14

Note: 1. The regional abbreviations denote the New England region, the Middle Atlantic Region, etc.

Table V.3. Flows of Electrical Energy Generated in 1990 by Region for the Monopoly Model (in Billions of kWh)

From/To	*NE*	*MA*	*ENC*	*WNC*	*SA*	*ESC*	*WSC*	*M*	*P*
1. NE	65.06								
2. MA		192.63							
3. ENC			262.56						
4. WNC				105.15					
5. SA					248.13				
6. ESC						142.53			
7. WSC							174.17		
8. M								57.79	
9. P									196.77

Table V.4. Investment in New Generating Capacity by Plant by Region for the Monopoly Model (in Billions of kWh)

Region	*Year*	*Hydroelectric Plants*	*Fossil-fueled Plants*	*Nuclear Plants*
1. New England	1990	3.41	0.0	14.66
2. Middle Atlantic	1990	21.46	0.0	0.0
3. East North Central	1990	19.55	0.0	48.02
4. West North Central	1990	3.70	0.0	26.42
5. South Atlantic	1990	9.84	0.0	61.85
6. East South Central	1990	14.52	0.0	0.0
7. West South Central	1990	0.0	0.0	47.96
8. Mountain	1990	0.0	0.0	0.0
9. Pacific	1990	0.5	0.0	0.0

dential sector on the average falls about 75 percent. For the commercial sector it falls about 40 percent, and for the industrial sector it falls about 90 percent. The monopoly price for 1975 is the range of 6.6 to 12.7 cents for the residential sector, in the range of 4.7 to 9.0 cents for the commercial sector, and in the range of 6.2 to 20.1 cents for the industrial sector. Needless to say, electrical energy pricing and allocation in 1975 did not closely resemble the pricing and allocation one would expect to find from a monopolist who completely controls the generation and pricing of electrical energy.

Continuing to use the perfect competition model of Chapters II and III as the norm, with the drastic reduction in the quantity demanded in the monopoly situation for all sectors and over the entire time period, the amount of investment in new generating capacity is sharply curtailed. Potential hydroelectric sites for the most part continue to be fully developed and utilized. The only exceptions being in a few of the regions in 1990. Beyond that, however, a limited amount of nuclear capacity and no fossil-fueled capacity is to be added. The major part of the generation of electrical energy will come from existing capacity. Note that the penalties incurred by society because of the limitations of hydroelectric plant additions to capacity are much less than they were in the case of perfect competition and are well nigh nonexistent for fossil-fueled plants and nuclear plants over the entire time period for all regions.

Summarily, by considering the foregoing monopoly model, it has been possible to look at briefly (1) the extent to which

Table V.5. Quasi-rent of a Plant by Region (in 0.1 cents per kWh).

Region	*Year*	*Hydroelectric Plants*	*Fossil-fueled Plants*	*Nuclear Plants*
1. New England	1975	7.65	0.0	0.0
	1990	2.19	0.0	0.0
2. Middle Atlantic	1975	8.20	0.0	0.0
	1990	3.00	0.0	0.0
3. East North Central	1975	8.07	0.0	0.0
	1990	2.70	0.0	0.0
4. West North Central	1975	7.27	0.0	0.0
	1990	1.76	0.0	0.0
5. South Atlantic	1975	6.77	0.0	0.07
	1990	1.23	0.0	0.0
6. East South Central	1975	7.42	0.0	0.0
	1990	2.04	0.0	0.0
7. West South Central	1975	5.54	0.0	0.09
	1990	0.0	0.0	0.0
8. Mountain	1975	5.44	0.0	0.0
	1990	0.0	0.0	0.0
9. Pacific	1975	0.0	0.0	0.0
	1990	0.0	0.0	0.0

society would be harmed (measured by a decrease in the value of net social welfare) if a central authority were to act as a monopolist pricing and allocating electrical energy and (2) the price and allocation profile that would result if this central authority were allowed to exist. While it is justifiable to conclude that the electrical energy industry on the whole does not act as a spatial monopolist, one cannot conclude that monopolistic tendencies are absent from the industry. Specifically, the industry does not satisfy the efficiency conditions since it does violate and is expected to continue violating the marginal cost pricing rule (see Chapter III).

THE REGULATED MONOPOLY

The electric utility industry in the United States does not operate as an unregulated monopolist. In fact, in the context of the three different types of regulatory limits on profits discussed in Chapter IV, the one limiting profit per unit of installed capacity (i.e., rate-of-return regulation) is typically applied by the state public utility commissions in the United States. Consequently, for the purposes here, only this rate-of-return regulatory constraint and its impact on price will be examined.

The critical parameter in this analysis is the fixed amount which a firm's earnings cannot exceed. Typically, this rate of return is expressed on a levelized basis as a percentage of the existing and new capacity. The percentage of relationships vary with ownership segments—privately owned, federal, municipal, and cooperative. They also vary by plant, primarily because of differences in service life of the units but also because of some difference in tax rates and other items. The allowed rates of return are calculated for each plant and vary regionally between 6.5 and 14.3 percent for hydroelectric plants, between 12.7 and 15.4 percent for fossil-fueled plants, and between 13.2 and 15.6 percent for nuclear plants.[5]

The profit-maximization problem can be solved again, but this time with the rate-of-return regulatory constraint imposed. As noted from the discussion in Chapter IV, one would expect to observe a lowering of the price to each consuming sector from the monopoly level as long as there is some positive addition to capacity, generation will be larger, and additions to capacity should increase. The quasi-rent of a plant will be unaffected. This is precisely the sequence that evolves as one looks at selected output values from the regulated monopoly model in Tables V.6 through V.9.

Table V.6. Average Regulated Monopoly Demand Price (in cents per kWh)[a]

Region	*1975*	*1990*
1. New England	4.04	5.61
2. Middle Atlantic	3.86	5.59
3. East North Central	2.61	3.83
4. West North Central	2.63	4.89
5. South Atlantic	2.93	5.01
6. East South Central	1.95	4.26
7. West South Central	2.05	5.65
8. Mountain	2.29	5.23
9. Pacific	2.12	5.08

Note: a. In constant 1975 dollars. Weighted price computed by weighting the contribution of each of the three consuming sectors to average price by its proportion of total demand.

Table V.7. Optimal Flows of Electrical Energy Generated in 1975 for the Regulated Monopoly Model (in Billions of kWh)

From/To	*NE*[1]	*MA*	*ENC*	*WNC*	*SA*	*ESC*	*WSC*	*M*	*P*
1. NE	76.93	6.10							
2. MA		223.80							
3. ENC			289.63						
4. WNC			26.27	118.61					
5. SA					236.61				
6. ESC					37.75	156.33			
7. WSC							198.43		
8. M								70.08	
9. P									222.39

Note: 1. NE denotes the New England region, MA denotes the Middle Atlantic region, and so forth.

Table V.8. Optimal Flows of Electrical Energy Generated in 1990 for the Regulated Monopoly Model (in Billions of kWh)

From/To	*NE*	*MA*	*ENC*	*WNC*	*SA*	*ESC*	*WSC*	*M*	*P*
1. NE	118.89								
2. MA		361.66							
3. ENC			487.97						
4. WNC				187.91					
5. SA					443.61				
6. ESC						259.42			
7. WSC							312.19		
8. M								93.94	
9. P									339.65

Table V.9. Optimal Investment in New Generating Capacity by Plant for the Monopoly Model (in Billions of kWh)

Region	*Year*	*Hydroelectric Plants*	*Fossil Plants*	*Nuclear Plants*
1. New England	1990	2.41	0.0	34.46
2. Middle Atlantic	1990	21.46	0.0	80.63
3. East North Central	1990	19.55	5.56	106.15
4. West North Central	1990	3.70	0.0	55.24
5. South Atlantic	1990	9.84	72.26	71.75
6. East South Central	1990	14.52	0.0	44.34
7. West South Central	1990	0.0	0.0	92.01
8. Mountain	1990	8.93	0.0	16.82
9. Pacific	1990	45.45	0.0	42.61

Average prices in each region in 1975 (not surprisingly) closely approximate the actual prices for that year. This is to be expected since the actual allowed rates of return were used in the calculation of the regulation constraint. Further, given the same allowed rates of return in the future, the average price of electrical energy will continue to be above the competitive equilibrium price through 1990. Since new capacity is being added in each of the periods considered, note that, uniformly, the price of electrical energy is below the unregulated monopoly level.

There is no suggestion of an Averch–Johnson bias. While capacity exceeds its monopoly level, it does not exceed the level dictated under the maximization of net social welfare criterion.

Also under the regulated monopoly case there are significant interregional flows of electrical energy in 1975 reflecting the differential costs of supplying electrical energy across regions. As in the perfect competition setting these flows fall to zero by 1990 as the regional cost disparities are eliminated.

SUMMARY

This chapter endeavored to investigate the impact of regulation on the pricing and allocation of electrical energy in the United States. The results were entirely consistent with the theoretical constructs presented in Chapter IV. Namely, under rate-of-return regulation, the optimal price of electrical energy will be below the unregulated monopoly level. Correspondingly, the capacity and net generation will exceed their unregulated monopoly levels as regulation has the effect of reducing monopoly profits from the unregulated level.

NOTES AND REFERENCES

1. E. M. Hoover, "Spatial Price Discrimination." *The Review of Economic Studies 4:* 182–191, 1937.
2. J. Henderson and R. E. Quandt, *Microeconomic Theory*, 2nd. ed. New York: McGraw Hill Book Company, 1971, pp. 164–267.
4. F. M. Scherer, *Industrial Market Structure and Economic Performance.* Chicago: Rand McNally and Company, 1970, p. 15.
4. R. E. Caves and R. W. Jones, *World Trade and Payments.* Boston: Little Brown and Company, 1973, pp. 206–210. This gives a diagrammatic exposition of the gains in welfare if one departs from a monopolistic structure and lets perfect competition prevail.
5. Federal Power Commission, *1970 National Power Survey.* Washington, D.C.: U.S. Government Printing Office, 1972.

Chapter VI

The Impact of Environmental Regulations on the Allocation and Pricing of Public Utility Service

INTRODUCTION

Recent years have witnessed a growing concern for the quality of the environment. Since the late 1960s, a variety of environmental quality standards have been actively discussed and implemented.[1] One of the important questions that has remained only partially answered about these options is the effect of their implementation on the pricing and allocation of energy, particularly electrical energy pricing and allocation.

Existing regulations as well as those adopted in the future, directly affect consumption through price increases resulting from the regulation of the emission of air pollutants from burning fossil fuels, thermal pollution, and the creation of noise. Thus, for example, all coal- and oil-fired generating plants of less than 200-MW capacity, and those with a 30 percent of less utilization factor are required to burn low sulfur by 1976.[2] Because low-sulfur fuel is more expensive,[3] the increase in fuel costs will reduce demand. Other types of controls will similarly affect costs. It is the effects of these regulations on the pricing and allocation of electrical energy that is the subject of this paper. The effects are investigated in the context of a peak-load pricing model.

The peak-loading pricing problem arises because the demand for electrical energy varies temporally (on a monthly, weekly, daily, and even hourly basis). Electrical energy in different periods is a typical example of a joint product. An input of equipment provides capacity in technically fixed (and in this case equal) proportions during each period. However, it is not necessary that production in each period should be equal to capacity. Further, an item of durable capital equipment provides capacity over its lifetime in fixed proportions (perhaps unequal if there is physical depreciation), but it will not necessarily be optimal to maintain production at full capacity.

The solution to the problem involves the allocation of the joint costs to the separate products. To accomplish this, an objective must be specified that is consistent with a set of operating criteria. The prime objective of electric utility operation is often stated as the maximization of net social welfare. The common expression for social welfare chosen, and the one to be used here, is given by total revenue plus consumer's surplus and social cost (treated as opportunity cost and assuming no technological externalities) and will be separable into total pecuniary cost less intramarginal rent. Assuming that all factors are available to the utility in completely elastic supply, intramarginal rents will be zero, and the net welfare is

$$\text{NSW} = \text{SB} - \text{SC} = \text{TR} + \text{CS} - \text{TC} \tag{6.1}$$

where NSW = net social welfare;
SB = social benefit;
SC = social cost;
TR = total revenue;
CS = consumer's surplus;
TC = total cost.

Underlying the analysis is the simplifying assumption that all of the optimum conditions of production and consumption are satisfied elsewhere in the economy. This is a strong assumption and potentially invalidates the analysis. An assumption such as this, however, is necessary to avoid the "second best" digressions.[4] This is merely an explicit statement of the usually implicit assumption in peak-load pricing formulations. Furthermore, since this assumption supplies the conditions permitting the employment of the theoretical apparatus of partial welfare economics to derive a benchmark, and further, since there is no well-specified alternative[5] (the claim that the assumptions are not satisfied needs to be articulated before it becomes useful), the analysis will proceed on this basis.

A solution to the peak-load or joint production pricing problem where several plants with differing costs to meet the demands exist can be found in Marshall's approach to joint product pricing. He explains that "If in equilibrium x′ oxen are annually supplied and sold at a price $y = \Phi(x)$; and each ox yields m units of beef; and if breeders find that by modifying the breeding and feeding of oxen they can increase their meat-yielding properties to the extent of Δm units of beef (the hide and other joint products being, on balance, unaltered) and the extra expense of doing this is $\Delta y'$, then $\Delta y'/\Delta m$ represents the marginal supply price of beef: if this price were less than the selling price, it would be to the interests of the breeders to make the change."[6]

The formulation of the problem here follows this approach of Marshall. In the problem specification, if the peak-period cost of using an additional plant θ is less than peak-period price when $\theta - 1$ plants are used, in line with the solution suggested by Marshall, it is beneficial to introduce plant θ.

The formulation of the peak-load pricing problem also rests on an assumption that the demand functions for electrical energy are known with certainty or are available in a certainty-equivalence sense[7] and that they are independent of each other. Two implications of this assumption are that the division into periods of equal duration presents no problem and that the demand curves are not stochastic. The combination of variable weather with a significant use of electrical energy for either space heating or air conditioning introduces an important stochastic element into electrical energy demand, since in addition to the regular daily and seasonal variations of these loads, there are also variations due to short-term weather changes. Prices should be varied to meet short-run fluctuations in demand induced by weather changes. Consumers, however, may prefer a simpler rate schedule which covers the cost of meeting a stochastically fluctuating demand. What they desire is both electrical energy and the right to use more if the weather changes for the worse. Consequently, utilities provide a margin of spare capacity to meet this occasional demand. This means that expected demand is less than available capacity. The magnitude of this margin depends on how much consumers value its availability. It will be assumed here that this margin is constant across all plants for all time periods.

THE ENVIRONMENT

Visualize a competitive economy where there is a demand for electrical energy and many generating plants of varying vintages and types and where the plants and consumers are spatially diffuse.[8] Before developing the model, it is convenient to introduce the following definitions and notation.

Let j,k = 1, 2, ..., R denote the regions;
θ = 1, 2, ..., P denote the generating plants;
i = 1, 2, ..., S denote the individual environmental quality standards;
t,τ = 1, 2, ..., T denote the discrete time periods of equal length;
y_{jt} = quantity of electrical energy demanded by consumers in region j in period t;
x^{θ}_{jt} = quantity of electrical energy generated by plant θ in region j in period t;
x_{jkt} = quantity of electrical energy transmitted from region j to region k in period t;
K^{θ}_{j1} = generating capacity of plant θ existing in region j in period 1;
I^{θ}_{jt} = investment in generating capacity of plant θ that will be available for operation in region j in period t;
$\hat{x}^{\theta}_{jst}$ = generation restrictions on plant θ in region j in period t imposed by specific environmental quality standards s;
$\hat{I}^{\theta}_{jt}$ = maximum investment in generating capacity of plant θ possible in region j in period t;
d_{jkt} = cost transmitting electrical energy from region j to region k plus (implicitly) cost of distributing it within region k in period t;
α^{θ}_{jt} = marginal cost of operation and maintenance (in-

cluding fuel cost) for plant θ in region j in period t;

β^{θ}_{jt} = marginal cost per unit of capacity (capital cost) for plant θ in region j in period t;

c^{θ}_{jst} = marginal cost of installing and maintaining environmental control equipment designed to meet the environmental quality standard s on plant θ in region j in period t (hereafter, explicit environmental quality costs);

r = interest rate.

Relying on the assumption that the demand functions for electrical energy are known with certainty or are available in the certainty equivalence sense, the demand functions are given in the form

$$p_{jt} = f_{jt}(y_{jt}), \tag{6.2}$$

where p_{jt} is the price of electrical energy in region j. Note that to simplify the analysis, only aggregate regional demand is considered. Individual consumers can be considered in a variant of the model.

The search for optimum demands, prices, and operating schedules is subject to several constraints:

1. For each region and each time period, the total quantity of electrical energy demanded is less than or equal to the quantity supplied by all regions:

$$y_{jt} \leq \sum_{k} x_{kjt}. \tag{6.3}$$

2. For each region and each time period, the total generation of electrical energy is less than or equal to the generation from all plants within that region:

$$\sum_{k} x_{jkt} \leq \sum_{\theta} x^{\theta}_{jt}. \tag{6.4}$$

3. For each plant in a region, generation is less than or equal to the generation from that generating capacity existing in the initial period plus the generation from capacity additions in the first and subsequent periods:

$$x^{\theta}_{jt} \leq K^{\theta}_{j1} + \sum_{\tau=1}^{t} I^{\theta}_{j\tau}. \tag{6.5}$$

There is a temptation to include a term accounting for the rate of decline of output over time due to "age." Since it is not significant for well-maintained plants, however, the concept is not included. Further, if capacity is not added in period t or that plant does not exist in the initial period, I^{θ}_{jt} or K^{θ}_{j} will be zero.

4. For each region, investment in generating capacity is constrained by physical, institutional, and technological limitations:

$$I^{\theta}_{jt} \leq \hat{I}^{\theta}_{jt}. \tag{6.6}$$

For example, it is well known that there is a maximum feasible expansion in, say, nuclear power development considering the constraints imposed by such things as licensing, development of additional uranium supplies, technical and construction manpower limitations, and difficulties with new and extrapolated equipment.[9]

Further, proposed locations for new generating plants are held up to environmental scrutiny and sites optimal in all respects may still be deemed environmentally unacceptable because it violates, say, the nonsignificant deterioration of the environment clause in the Clean Air Act.[10] The cancellation of the new coal-fired plant proposed for the Kaiparowits Plateau in Southern Utah is a most recent example of the limitations of capacity additions arising from environmental considerations.

Additionally, given that the problem is marked at an initial point (i.e., t = 1), capacity additions in this period are nonexistent:

$$I^{\theta}_{j1} = 0. \tag{6.6a}$$

Note that this constraint is subsumed in constraint (6.5).

5. For any plant in a region in a specific period, output might be limited to control for environmental effects:

$$x^{\theta}_{jt} \leq \hat{x}^{\theta}_{jst}. \tag{6.7}$$

This constraint needs elaboration. It is potentially desirable during a specific period or periods during the day to control the volume of atmospheric pollutants emanating from a given plant. By limiting output, the pollutants can be controlled. Thus, sulfur emissions from fossil plants might be severely restricted during the periods when automobile pollution is at its maximum, i.e., during rush hour. Alternatively, complaints of nuisance-type noise from residents near the boundaries of generating plants have been problems which electric utilities have faced for years. The noise level can be controlled by controlling output.[11]

Before proceeding, a number of points need to be clarified concerning the economic environment:

1. Additions to capacity are looked upon as an average. To include a margin of spare capacity required to meet demands above the mean expectation, I_{jt}^{θ} can be inflated by the appropriate margin.
2. There is no discussion of terminal conditions. This does not preclude such discussions in a variant of the model.
3. The formulation is deterministic. Accounting for uncertainties in demand, plant availability, and so forth can be included in the margin of spare capacity factor.
4. Attention is focused on the basic economic aspects of the problem with no attention being paid to all sorts of practical engineering aspects. It must be recognized that this model use is the first of several stages of the investment decision process. The search for a solution that satisfies economic and social criteria is an iterative process.

PRODUCTION OVER TIME

It is now possible to form the total net social welfare function. Using the notation as defined, the Hotelling type[12] of net social welfare which forms the objective function of the problem may be characterized as

$$\mathrm{NSW} = \sum_{t} \sigma^{t-1} \Bigg[\sum_{j} \int f_{jt}(y_{jt}) \; dy_{jt} - \sum_{j} \sum_{\theta} \alpha_{jt}^{\theta} x_{jt}^{\theta} - \sum_{j} \sum_{\theta} \sum_{s} c_{jst}^{\theta} x_{jt}^{\theta} - \sum_{j} \sum_{\theta} \beta_{jt}^{\theta} I_{jt}^{\theta} - \sum_{j} \sum_{k} d_{jkt} x_{jkt} \Bigg] \qquad (6.8)$$

where $\sigma^{t-1} = \dfrac{1}{(1+r)^{t-1}}$.

Providing the demand functions are downward sloping, the objective function is concave, and the Kuhn–Tucker conditions[13] will give the necessary and sufficient conditions for optimality. Associating the dual variables $\sigma^{t-1}\lambda_{1jt}$, $\sigma^{t-1}\lambda_{2jt}$, $\sigma^{t-1}\mu_{\theta jt}$, $\sigma^{t-1}\rho_{\theta jt}$, $\sigma^{t-1}\lambda^{\theta}_{jst}$ with constraints (6.3) and (6.7), respectively, and multiplying throughout by σ^{t-1} where appropriate, the Kuhn–Tucker conditions are

$$y_{jt} \leq \sum_{k} x_{kjt} \qquad \lambda_{1jt} \geq 0 \tag{6.9}$$

$$\sum_{k} x_{jkt} \leq \sum_{\theta} x^{\theta}_{jt} \qquad \lambda_{2jt} \geq 0 \tag{6.10}$$

$$x^{\theta}_{jt} \leq K^{\theta}_{j1} + \sum_{\tau=1}^{t} I^{\theta}_{j\tau} \qquad \mu_{\theta jt} \geq 0 \tag{6.11}$$

$$I^{\theta}_{jt} \leq \hat{I}^{\theta}_{jt} \qquad \rho_{\theta jt} \geq 0 \tag{6.12}$$

$$x^{\theta}_{jt} \leq \hat{x}^{\theta}_{jst} \qquad \lambda^{\theta}_{jst} \geq 0 \tag{6.13}$$

$$f_{jt}(y_{jt}) \leq \lambda_{1jt} \qquad y_{jt} \geq 0 \tag{6.14}$$

$$\lambda_{1kt} \leq d_{jkt} + \lambda_{2jt} \qquad x_{jkt} \geq 0 \tag{6.15}$$

$$\lambda_{2jt} \leq \alpha^{\theta}_{jt} + \sum_{s} c^{\theta}_{jst} + \mu_{\theta jt} + \lambda^{\theta}_{js^*t} \qquad x^{\theta}_{jt} \geq 0 \tag{6.16}$$

$$\sum_{t' \geq t} \sigma^{t'-t}\mu_{\theta jt'} \leq \beta^{\theta}_{jt} + \rho_{\theta jt} \qquad I^{\theta}_{jt} \geq 0. \tag{6.17}$$

$\mu_{\theta jt}$ can be interpreted as the quasi-rent of plant θ in region j in period t and, if that plant is utilized, is equal to the supply price minus the marginal operation and maintenance cost (hereafter, operating cost), the sum of the explicit costs of each of the environmental quality standards $\Sigma_s\, c^{\theta}_{jst}$, and the implicit cost of the environmental quality standards $\lambda^{\theta}_{js^*t}$. Thus, if

$$x^{\theta}_{jt} > 0, \qquad \text{then } \mu_{\theta jt} = \lambda_{2jt} - \left(\alpha^{\theta}_{jt} + \sum_{s} c^{\theta}_{jst} + \lambda^{\theta}_{js^*t}\right). \tag{6.16a}$$

Note that almost only one of the capacity constraints arising from environmental quality standards giving rise to the implicit cost is binding at any particular time in a given region. The binding constraint is denoted by s*.

Supposing in addition $y_{jt} > 0$ and $x_{jkt} > 0$, the quasi-rent will be exactly equal to the market demand price λ_{1jt} less the sum of the marginal costs.

To minimize total cost, generation will be scheduled on equipment in increasing order of operating cost plus the explicit costs of the environmental quality standards plus transmission cost. Therefore, the demand price in any period t in region j equals the sum of these costs on the least-efficient plant in any region k, denoted by ϕ, being used to generate electrical energy. Thus, if

$$0 < x^{\phi}_{kt} < K^{\phi}_{k1} + \sum_{\tau=1}^{t} I^{\phi}_{kt},$$

then

$$f_{jt}(y_{jt}) = \alpha^{\phi}_{kt} + \sum_{s} c^{\phi}_{kst} + d_{kjt} \qquad (6.11a)$$

provided $x^{\theta}_{kt} < \hat{x}^{\theta}_{kst}$ for all s.

The quasi-rent of any plant is equal to the difference between the sum of its operating cost, implicit and explicit environmental quality costs and delivery costs and those of the least-efficient plant. Thus, if

$$x^{\phi}_{jt} > 0, \qquad \text{then } \mu_{\phi jt} = \alpha^{\phi}_{jt} + \sum_{s} c^{\phi}_{jst} + d^{\phi}_{kjt} - \left(\alpha^{\theta}_{jt} + \sum_{s} c^{\theta}_{jst} + d_{kjt}\right), \qquad (6.18)$$

where d^{ϕ}_{kjt} denotes the delivery cost from the least-efficient plant.

Observe that it is possible to use a plant to generate electrical energy that does not have the lowest operating cost. If the transmission (as well as distribution) cost is sufficiently large, then it might be optimal to use a plant with higher combined operating and environmental quality costs while shutting down a more efficient one.

The relations (6.11a) and (6.16a) indicate effects on price of the imposition of environmental quality standards. The price of electrical energy to the consumer in period t in region j will increase by the explicit cost of the environmental quality standards $\Sigma_s c^{\theta}_{jst}$ plus the implicit cost $\lambda^{\theta}_{js^*t}$.[14] The value of the explicit cost can be computed simply from the knowledge of, say, the operating cost of cooling towers per kilowatt-hour (about .05 mills/kWh) or the operating cost for the limestone scrubbing (about .34 mills/kWh).[2] The implicit cost, the cost of electrical energy due to the restriction of generation from a particular plant, cannot a priori be calculated. It is dependent on the level of the capacity constraint for the particular plant, total system demand for electrical energy, and generation constraints on other plants. Thus, for example, if a given plant is the most efficient in all respects (based on an operating cost and explicit environmental quality cost criterion), but it is required to forego all generation during a particular period, the implicit cost in this period for this plant would equal the difference between its operating cost plus explicit environmental cost and these costs for the next most efficient plant.

Additions to capacity are undertaken on the basis of a least-cost criterion. New capacity (either an additional plant or an expansion of an existing plant) should be added in any period up to the point where the discounted sum of its quasi-rents equals the purchase price plus the marginal value of a particular plant addition (or quasi-rent because the capacity expansion is limited either by technological or environmental considerations). Thus, if

$$I_{jt} > 0, \qquad \text{then} \sum_{t'>t} \sigma^{t'-t}\mu_{\theta jt'} < \beta^{\theta}_{jt} + \rho_{\theta jt}. \qquad (6.17a)$$

The pricing implications of prohibiting capacity expansion in a particular region can be seen by focusing on, say, period t, when it would have been optimal to build a plant in region j, but it must be built in region k because of environmental prohibitions. The increase in the price of electrical energy, measured by the quasi-rent $\rho_{\theta jt}$, will equal the difference between total costs including capital cost, operating cost, explicit and implicit environmental costs, and delivery cost for the plant that is built and these costs for the plant that was prohibited.

The quasi-rent of a plant in any period can be regarded as that part of the supply price set aside to cover depreciation and interest on capital. This is what Turvey calls *amortization.*[15] If new capacity is added in any period, and if the maximum capacity addition is not reached, demand price in that period is equal to operating cost plus amortization on the new plant plus explicit and implicit environmental costs plus transmission cost. Thus, denoting the new plant by n, if

$$x^{n}_{kt} > 0 \qquad y_{jt} > 0,$$

then

$$f_{jt}(y_{jt}) = \alpha^{n}_{kt} + \mu_{nkt} + \sum_{s} c^{n}_{kst} + \lambda^{n}_{ks^{*}t} + d_{kjt} \tag{6.19}$$

A plant m should begin to be retired when its operating cost and environmental quality costs rise above the level of the operating cost plus amortization plus environmental quality costs of the new plant (given transmission cost is the same). Thus, if

$$\alpha^{m}_{kt} + \sum c^{m}_{kst} + \lambda^{m}_{ks^{*}t} > \alpha^{n}_{kt} + \mu_{nkt} + \sum_{s} c^{n}_{kst} + \lambda^{n}_{ks^{*}t},$$

then

$$x^{m}_{kt} = 0. \tag{6.20}$$

The implications of this are that a sufficiently high combination of costs to meet environmental quality standards will force the retirement of existing generating capacity before what otherwise would have been optimal.

Equation (6.17a) can be interpreted to mean that the present value of amortization equals the purchase price of new capacity plus the quasi-rent of the capacity limitation. Consequently, the present value of total profit is zero. The issue to be emphasized is that the amount set aside for amortization varies from period to period depending on demand and perhaps is equal to zero in some periods. With demand varying, a constant proportion of capacity cost each period should not necessarily be recouped. Rather, price should be set to just fully utilize capacity (conditional upon price not being below marginal production cost and the cost of meeting environmental quality standards), and capacity should be selected so that over the life of the plant, capacity cost is just recouped.

ANALYSIS OF THE MODEL

By casting the problem in a spatial dimension as well as the temporal dimension, the way has been open to handling many of the knotty problems with investment in generating capacity as well as the problems involved with price adjustment and allocation over time as such things as stricter environmental quality standards in conjunction with technological change permitting the cheaper transmission of electrical energy over long distances become realistic.

The general principles of optimal pricing from this model can be summarized as follows:

1. Set prices by time of day (or seasons of the year) in accordance with the pattern of demand. This means that any customer in a particular hour be treated the same regardless of how much they consume.
2. Charge high prices when the quantity demanded rises above the level of capacity. Thus, a utility can obtain a quasi-rent in the short run by charging a price in excess of the operating, capital, environmental, and transmission costs. This ignores the longer run consideration of imposing a penalty on the utility due to inadequate capacity to meet future requirements.
3. Vary prices spatially depending on how far the consumer is from the generating plant.
4. Capital costs are imputed to consumers only to the extent their demand presses on the capacity of a generating plant. Thus, any increase in demand during a peak period requiring a utility to expand its generating capacity will result in a charge for electrical energy just sufficient to compensate for the increased cost associated with satisfying demand.
5. Require consumers to bear the implicit and explicit costs of implementing environmental quality standards.

The impact of environmental quality standards will vary from one time period to another and from one region to another depending upon the plants used and the standards imposed in any particular region during the time interval of interest. With an increase in the price of electrical energy resulting as the consumer is required to bear these costs, the aggregate effect will be dependent on the reduction in output which in turn is dependent on the demand elasticities in each time period.

Environmental regulation has an impact on the price of

electrical energy where the objective is profit maximization as well as under a welfare-maximizing objective. What differs in the two situations is that under profit maximization, price exceeds rather than equals a summation of the various marginal costs. When regulation is imposed, there will be price reductions as output is moved closer to the welfare-maximizing level. This is the focus of the following sections.

PRODUCTION WITH PROFIT MAXIMIZATION

Assume that the objective is the maximization of profit π. The objective function of the problem may now be characterized as

$$\pi = \sum_t \sigma^{t-1} \Bigg[\sum_j f_{jt}(y_{jt})y_{jt} - \sum_j \sum_\theta \alpha_{jt}^\theta x_{jt}^\theta - \sum_j \sum_\theta \sum_s c_{jst}^\theta x_{jt}^\theta - \sum_j \sum_\theta \beta_{jt}^\theta I_{jt}^\theta - \sum_j \sum_k d_{jkt} x_{jkt} \Bigg]. \tag{6.21}$$

Providing the demand functions are downward sloping, the objective function is concave, and the Kuhn-Tucker conditions will give the necessary and sufficient conditions for optimality. Associating the dual variably with constraints (6.3) through (6.7) as before, the Kuhn-Tucker conditions can be derived.

Instead of Eq. (6.14), one now has

$$y_{jt}f'_{jt}(y_{jt}) + f_{jt}(y_{jt}) \leq \lambda_{1jt} \qquad y_{jt} \geq 0. \tag{6.14a}$$

The rest of the conditions are the same as before.

Assuming a positive quantity of electrical energy is demanded, it follows that

$$\lambda_{1jt} = \frac{\partial}{\partial_{yt}} [f_{jt}(y_{jt})y_{jt}], \tag{6.22}$$

or λ_{1jt} is equal to the marginal revenue in region j in period t.

Consequently, the essential difference between an unregulated profit maximizing objective and the welfare-maximizing objective is that the dual variable λ_{1jt} must be regarded as marginal revenue and the price set accordingly in the former instance, whereas it is the price to the consumer in the latter instance.

PRODUCTION SUBJECT TO REGULATORY CONSTRAINT

Now introduce a regulatory limit which holds profit at or below some level which will generally increase as the size of the system is increased. Three particular forms of the profit ceiling will be considered.

The first method of regulation limits profits to a fixed amount per unit of output. Thus, profits are equal to some fraction of a cent per kilowatt-hour, γ, such that

$$\pi^{\theta}_{1jt} \leq \gamma x^{\theta}_{jt}, \tag{6.23}$$

where π^{θ}_{1jt} is the maximum profit on the generation by plant θ in region j in period t.

Combining this regulatory constraint with the profit maximization means maximizing Eq. (6.21) subject to constraints (6.3) through (6.7) and (6.23).

Making the same assumption with regard to the demand functions and associating the dual variables as before and associating the dual variable $\sigma^{t-1}\eta_{\theta jt}$ with constraint (6.23), the Kuhn-Tucker conditions can be obtained. All of them will be the same with the exception of Eq. (6.11) as noted before and condition (6.16) which becomes

$$\lambda_{2jt} \leq \alpha^{\theta}_{jt} + \sum_{s} c^{\theta}_{jst} + \mu_{\theta jt} + \lambda^{\theta}_{js^{*}t} - \eta_{\theta jt} \qquad x^{\theta}_{jt} \geq 0 \tag{6.16b}$$

and the addition of

$$\pi^{\theta}_{1jt} \leq \gamma x^{\theta}_{jt} \qquad \eta_{\theta jt} \geq 0. \tag{6.24}$$

Condition (6.16b) is the one with significant regulatory implications. When the quantity of electrical energy generated by a particular plant in a particular region is positive, the marginal cost will equal the marginal operating cost plus explicit and implicit environmental costs plus the quasi-rent for the particular plant less the marginal profitability of an additional unit of output. Since the latter term (in all probability) is positive, the marginal cost will be lower. Hence, given positive generation from this plant, a lower marginal revenue is implied and, with a downward-sloping demand curve, this means a larger output with a lower price. Thus, under regulation limiting profit per unit of output, any output will result in a lower marginal revenue than in the unregulated case. All consumers benefit equally. Finally, because the return is applied uniformly to every unit of output, the sequence in which generating units are brought into operation (i.e., by the least-cost criterion) will not be altered from the welfare-maximization situation.

A second method of regulation permits a fair return on total cost. Denoting the fair return by ν, one has

$$\pi_{2t} \leq \nu \Bigg(\sum_{j} \sum_{\theta} \alpha_{jt}^{\theta} x_{jt}^{\theta} + \sum_{j} \sum_{\theta} \sum_{s} c_{jst}^{\theta} x_{jt}^{\theta} + \sum_{j} \sum_{\theta} \beta_{jt}^{\theta} I_{jt}^{\theta} + \sum_{j} \sum_{k} d_{jkt} x_{jkt} \Bigg), \tag{6.25}$$

where π_{2t} is the profit on total costs in period t.

It is a straightforward matter to associate the dual variable $\sigma^{t-1}\xi_t$ with this constraint and proceed as before. Going through the mathematics of the argument, it can be shown that regulation utilizing a fair-return-on-total-cost criterion will reduce marginal revenue by the same amount for all plants, all regions, and all time periods. The result will be analogous to that observed with the previous criterion.

A third method of regulation, and the one most widely used, utilizes a return-on-investment criterion. Under this method, total earnings in a period may not exceed a fixed amount, ε, for each unit of installed capacity so that

$$\pi_{3jt}^{\theta} \leq \varepsilon \left(K_{j1}^{\theta} + \sum_{\tau=1}^{t} I_{j\tau}^{\theta} \right), \tag{6.26}$$

where π_{3jt}^{θ} is the profit on one unit of installed capacity on plant θ in region j in period t.

Assuming that profit maximization is the objective and that constraint (6.26) is added to constraints (6.3) through (6.7), the optimality conditions can be derived. For downward-sloping demand functions and the dual variables defined as before and for the dual variable $\sigma^{t-1}\omega_{jt}^{\theta}$ associated with constraint (6.26), the Kuhn–Tucker conditions are the same with exception of Eq. (6.11) as noted and relation (6.17), which becomes

$$\sum_{t' \geq t} \sigma^{t'-t} \mu_{\theta jt'} \leq \beta_{jt}^{\theta} + \rho_{\theta jt} - \varepsilon \sum_{t' \geq t} \sigma^{t'-t} \omega_{jt'}^{\theta}, \tag{6.17a}$$

and the addition of

$$\pi^{\theta}_{3jt} \leq \varepsilon \left(K^{\theta}_{j1} + \sum_{\tau=1}^{t} I^{\theta}_{j\tau} \right) \qquad \omega^{\theta}_{jt} \geq 0. \tag{6.27}$$

This says as before that additions to capacity are undertaken on the basis of a least-cost criterion. Now, however, new capacity should be added in any period up to the point where the discounted sum of its quasi-rents equals the purchase price plus the marginal value of a particular plant addition in a particular region minus the discounted sum of the marginal profitability of a particular plant addition. This latter term can be regarded as that part of the supply price set aside to provide a fair rate of return on investment for each unit of generating capacity.

In this case, regulation will result in a lowering of the price from the profit-maximization level so long as capacity expansion is positive. This will happen because the quasi-rent of a plant will be lower in any period (lower by the marginal profitability). With a lower quasi-rent, total marginal costs will be adjusted downward. Equating marginal revenue to this lower marginal cost results in a larger output at a lower price. Thus, the regulator achieves the goal that output is increased from the profit-maximization level.

It is possible that this adjusted marginal cost will be sufficiently lower that capacity will be larger than the level required were price equated to actual marginal cost. One is observing with this method of regulation the Averch–Johnson effect.[16] There will be an overbuilding of capacity because profits increase with the level of capacity. The firm will pass along the benefits of regulation to those consumers whose increased demand causes an increase in capacity.

The expansion of capacity and the size of the fair rate of return ε are related in a predictable way. Namely, the closer the fair rate is to the cost of capital, the larger will be the capacity. This can be seen by observing that the quasi-rent of a plant in a particular region is lower the closer the cost of capital is to the rate of return, and thus by condition (6.17a) the indicated result is obtained.

Environmental quality standards will have an impact to the extent that the rate of return ε is adjusted to compensate the utility for the added cost of installing and maintaining equipment to meet the environmental quality standards. By singling out certain types of capital equipment, for example, pollution abatement devices, for specialized treatment, the increased rate-of-return will affect a lower adjusted marginal cost that yields a lower marginal revenue in peak periods and consequently a still larger investment in new capacity.

A comparison of the various methods of regulation shows that the method of regulation can have a substantial effect on the distribution of price reductions between consumers inducing an expansion in capacity and those utilizing only existing capacity. Under rate-of-return regulation, price reductions are realized only by peak-period consumers. Capacity is expanded from the profit-maximizing level toward (and perhaps even past) the economically optimal (price equal to marginal cost) level. This method of regulation thus provides an advantage in that it dampens the monopolistic tendency to restrict output, but it also entails the disadvantage that off-peak consumers do not share in the price reductions. This latter problem is corrected by the alternative methods of constraint. Under regulation limiting profit per unit output, all consumers share in price reductions regardless of whether they utilize new capacity or previously existing capacity. The rule for regulation limiting return on costs is that the same percentage decrease in marginal revenue be given in peak as in off-peak periods. Under all three constraints, regulation is effective in that monopoly profits are reduced from the unregulated level and generating capacity is larger.

CONCLUSION

In the foregoing analysis the effects of environmental regulation on the pricing and allocation of electrical energy have been discussed. In the situation where the maximization of social welfare was the objective, price in any period in a region is set equal to the operating cost, explicit and implicit environmental quality costs, amortization on new capacity if new capacity is added in that period, and delivery cost. A sufficiently high combination of costs to meet enviornmental quality standards will result in the earlier retirement of existing generating capacity than otherwise would have been optimal.

With a profit-maximization objective where profit is subject to a return-on-investment constraint, the imposition of environmental quality standards will lead via the Averch–Johnson effect to a larger investment in new generating capacity provided the cost of installing equipment to meet environmental quality standards is included in the rate of return.

NOTES AND REFERENCES

1. Culminating in the Clean Air Amendments of 1970 and Federal Water Pollution Control Amendments of 1972.
2. Council on Environmental Quality, *The Economic Impact of Pollution Control.* Washington, D.C.: U.S. Government Printing Office, 1972, pp. 98–99.
3. For example, see Federal Power Commission, *National Power Survey: Environmental Research.* Washington, D.C.: U.S. Government Printing Office, 1974.
4. O. E. Williamson, "Peak Load Pricing and Optimal Pricing Under Indivisibility Constraints." *The American Economic Review 56:* 810–827, 1966.
5. N. D. Uri, *Towards An Efficient Allocation of Electrical Energy.* Lexington, Mass.: D. C. Heath, 1975.
6. A. Marshall, *Principles of Economics,* 9th (Variorum) Ed. London: MacMillan Ltd., 1920.
7. H. Theil, *Optimal Decision Rules for Government and Industry.* Amsterdam: North-Holland Publishing Company, 1964.
8. To properly formulate the problem the notation must change slightly from that previously used. Focus is directed to specific plant types (hydroelectric, conventional coal, oil, natural gas, nuclear, etc.) as opposed to a general plant.
9. Joint Committee on Atomic Energy, *Understanding the "National Energy Dilemma.* Washington, D.C.: U.S. Government Printing Office, 1973.
10. Environmental Protection Agency, *The Clean Air Act,* processed, December 1970.
11. Federal Power Commission, *Air Pollution and the Regulated Electric Power and Natural Gas Industries,* processed, September 1978.
12. H. Hotelling, "The General Welfare in Relation to Problems of Taxation and of Railway and Utility Rates." *Econometrica 6:* 242–269, 1938.
13. H. W. Kuhn and A. W. Tucker, "Nonlinear Programming," in J. Neyman (ed.), *Proceedings of the Second Berkeley Symposium on Mathematical Statistics and Probability.* Berkeley: University of California Press, 1951, pp. 481–492.
14. Assuming that plant θ is being used to generate electrical energy and that it is the least efficient one in operation in period t.
15. R. Turvey, "Marginal Cost." *The Economic Journal LXXIX:* 282–299, 1969.
16. H. Averch and L. Johnson, "Behavior of the Firm Under Regulatory Constraint." *The American Economic Review 52:* 1053–1069, 1962.

Chapter VII

Optimal Pricing: A Different Perspective

INTRODUCTION

This chapter provides an analysis of the optimal pricing problem when a series of efficiency constraints are imposed instead of the heretofore used regulatory criteria (used in Chapters IV and VI). As alluded to previously (Chapter I), considerable controversy surrounds the use of the normative concept of net social welfare. This exposition attempts to mitigate some of the dispute. Because the nature of the solution in its simplest form is quite complex, no spatial considerations are introduced. The results, however, are applicable to both (the spatial and the temporal) dimensions.

The solution to the problem involves the allocation of the joint costs to the separate products. To accomplish this, an objective must be specified that is consistent with a set of operating criteria. The prime objective of electric utility operation is often stated as the maximization of social welfare. That this is a goal to be desired, few would question; that it cannot be translated directly into operational criterion for system operation, few would deny. Translation requires not only agreement on a definition for the deceptively simple phrase "social welfare" but also some assurance that the concept as defined is measurable. For these reasons the common expression chosen for social welfare is gross benefit less total cost which is equivalent to consumer's surplus plus total revenue less total cost. Consumer's surplus is simply the differences between what a consumer would be willing to pay for a good or service and what they actually pay.

A convenient formulation for the multidimensional consumer's surplus with dependent demand functions is given by Hotelling.[1] If one considers a set of unrelated commodities whose demand functions are

$$\overline{P}_i = P_i(q_1, q_2, ..., q_n) \qquad i = 1, 2, ..., n, \tag{7.1}$$

then the formulation is of the form

$$\int_c (P_1\, dq_1 + P_2\, dq_2 + \cdots + P_n\, dq_n) - \sum_{i=1}^{n} \overline{P}_i \overline{q}_i \tag{7.2}$$

with the integration being performed along some curve c and $\overline{P}_i$ and $\overline{q}_i$ being the equilibrium price and quantity.

There are two difficulties with this formulation. First, the necessary conditions for a local maximum or minimum of a real function require that the first derivatives of that function vanish at all critical points. Since the consumer's surplus is a part of the objective function which is to be optimized, the differentiability of consumer's surplus is required if classical optimization techniques are to be used. Second, consumer's surplus, as it is defined, depends on the particular path c chooses and is thus not unique.

Both problems can be solved by introducing a theorem on line integrals that states that if a set of integrability conditions are assumed, the coefficients of substitution or complementarity of any pair of goods (i and k) must equal the corresponding pair (k and i) of demand functions, i.e.,

$$\frac{\partial P_i}{\partial q_k} = \frac{\partial p_k}{\partial q_i}, \tag{7.3}$$

then a line integral of the form of relation (7.2) is differentiable, and the value of the consumer's surplus is independent of the path c.[2] Thus, in order to accept the results of the peak load pricing solution based on the Hotelling formulation of consumer's surplus, the integrability conditions (7.3) need to be assumed.

The viability of this assumption is empirical not theoretical. If one derives the system of demand functions from a utility function, direct or indirect, there is no problem of integrability—

although there may still be restrictions on the set of demand functions.[3] The integrability problem arises if the point of departure of the analysis is the system of demand functions rather than the direct or the indirect utility functions.[4] There is no reason why integrability should be expected to hold with aggregate data (aggregated across individuals). With aggregate data, the conditions for integrability are extremely restrictive: either the preferences of all individuals are all identical and homothetic, or the preferences and incomes of all individuals are identical. In practice, neither of these two conditions are likely to hold. In fact recent work has resulted in the rejection of the hypothesis of integrability.[5] Some reasons include the error in aggregation across individuals (failure to take into account the changing distribution of income), the possibility of taste differences across individuals at any one time, and the error in ignoring dynamic considerations (habit formation, stock adjustment, etc.).

With a rejection of the hypothesis of integrability, where does this leave us? The common expression for social welfare must be rejected and an alternative inserted in its place. Whether the operating criteria will change as a result remains to be seen. This is the objective of this chapter.

A WELFARE MAXIMIZATION APPROACH TO MARGINAL-COST PRICING WITH JOINT COSTS

As a point of departure, the various operating rules resulting from the traditional approach to the problem will be illustrated. It will be assumed that we are not concerned with terminal conditions. This assumption is made solely for ease of explication and will not alter the development of the argument and the consequent results. For each time period t up to a fixed horizon T, let

y_t = quantity of electrical energy demanded;
$f_t(y_t)$ = demand function;
x_t^θ = production on equipment of vintage θ;
x_t = total supply;
c_t^θ = marginal operation and maintenance cost (hereafter, operating cost) on equipment of vintage θ;
W_t = purchase of new equipment;

ξ_t = marginal purchase price of equipment;
r = rate of interest.

Present value of consumer's surplus plus total revenue less total cost, which is to be maximized, is given by

$$\sum_{t=1}^{T} \sigma^{t-1} \left[\int f_t(y_t)\, dy_t - \sum_{\theta=1}^{t} c_t^\theta x_t^\theta - \xi_t W_t \right], \tag{7.4}$$

where $\sigma^{t-1} = \dfrac{1}{(1 + r)^{t-1}}$.

The system operation is subject to several constraints:

1. Total quantity demanded must be less than or equal to the total supply

$$y_t \leq x_t \qquad t = 1, 2, ..., T. \tag{7.5}$$

2. Total supply is less than or equal to the sum of production on equipment of all vintages

$$x_t \leq \sum_{\theta=1}^{t} x_t^\theta \qquad t = 1, 2, ..., T. \tag{7.6}$$

3. For each vintage of equipment, production cannot exceed capacity

$$x_t^\theta \leq W_\theta \qquad t = \theta, \theta + 1, ..., T \text{ and } \theta = 1, 2, ..., T. \tag{7.7}$$

Now associate the dual variables $\sigma^{t-1}\rho_{1t}$, $\sigma^{t-1}\rho_{2t}$, and $\sigma^{t-1}\rho_t^\theta$ with constraints (7.5), (7.6), and (7.7), respectively.

Providing the demand curves are downward sloping, the objective function (7.4) is concave, and the Kuhn-Tucker conditions will give the necessary and sufficient conditions for a competitive solution. Multiplying through by σ^{t-1} where appropriate, the Kuhn-Tucker conditions are

$$y_t \leq x_t \qquad \rho_{1t} \geq 0 \tag{7.8}$$

$$x_t \leq \sum_{\theta=1}^{t} x_t^\theta \qquad \rho_{2t} \geq 0 \tag{7.9}$$

$$x_t^\theta \leq W_\theta \qquad \rho_t^\theta \geq 0 \tag{7.10}$$

$$\rho_{1t} \leq \rho_{2t} \qquad x_t \geq 0 \qquad (7.11)$$

$$f_t(y_t) \leq \rho_{1t} \qquad y_t \geq 0 \qquad (7.12)$$

$$\rho_{2t} \leq c_t^\theta + \rho_t^\theta \qquad x_t^\theta \geq 0 \qquad (7.13)$$

$$\sum_{t' \geq t} \sigma^{t'-t} \rho_{t'}^\theta \leq \xi_t \qquad W_t \geq 0. \qquad (7.14)$$

ρ_t^θ can be interpreted as the quasi-rent of equipment of vintage θ in period t and, if that equipment is utilized, is equal to supply price minus marginal operating cost. Thus, if

$$x_t^\theta > 0, \qquad \text{then } \rho_t^\theta = \rho_{2t} - c_t^\theta. \qquad (7.13a)$$

Supposing in addition $y_t > 0$ and $x_t > 0$, the quasi-rent will be exactly equal to the market demand price ρ_{1t} less the operating cost. If the equipment is not fully utilized, $x_t^\theta < W_\theta$, then its quasi-rent is zero. Thus, if

$$x_t^\theta < W_\theta, \qquad \text{then } \rho_t^\theta = 0. \qquad (7.10a)$$

To minimize total cost, production will be scheduled on equipment in increasing order of marginal operating cost. Thus, once again assuming $y_t > 0$ and $x_t > 0$, the demand price in any period t equals marginal operating cost on the least efficient equipment then in use whose vintage is denoted by θ^*. Thus, if

$$0 < x_t^{\theta^*} < W_{\theta^*}, \qquad \text{then } f_t(y_t) = c_t^{\theta^*}. \qquad (7.15)$$

The quasi-rent of any equipment in use is in fact the difference between its marginal operating cost and that of the least efficient equipment then in operation. Thus, if

$$x_t^\theta > 0, \qquad \text{then } \rho_t^\theta = c_t^{\theta^*} - c_t^\theta \qquad (7.16)$$

conditional upon y_t and x_t being positive.

Equipment should be purchased in any period up to the point where the discounted sum of its quasi-rents equals marginal purchase price. Thus, if

$$W_\theta > 0, \qquad \text{then } \sum_{t' \geq t} \sigma^{t'-t} \rho_{t'}^\theta = \xi_t \qquad (7.14a)$$

The quasi-rent of equipment in any period t can be regarded as that part of the output price set aside to cover depreciation and interest on capital. This is what Turvey[6] called *amortization*. If new equipment is purchased in any period, demand price in that period is equal to marginal operating cost plus amortization on the new equipment. Thus, if

$$x_t^\theta > 0, \qquad y_t > 0, \qquad \text{then} \quad f_t(y_t) = c_t^t + \rho_t^t. \tag{7.17}$$

Equipment of vintage θ should begin to be retired when its marginal operating cost rises above this level. Thus, if

$$c_t^\theta > c_t^t + \rho_t^t, \qquad \text{then} \quad x_t^\theta = 0. \tag{7.18}$$

Equation (7.14a) can be interpreted to mean that present value of amortization equals the purchase price of equipment. Consequently, the present value of total profit is zero. The issue to be emphasized is that the amount set aside for amortization varies from period to period depending on demand and perhaps is equal to zero in some periods. With demand varying, a constant proportion of capacity cost each period should not necessarily be recouped. Rather, price should be set to just fully utilize capacity (conditional upon price not being below marginal production cost), and capacity should be selected so that over the life of the equipment, capacity cost is just recouped.

The foregoing then are the operating criteria for a public utility maximizing social welfare defined in expression (7.4). All of the results are conditional upon the integrability conditions obtaining. With the dubious validity of these conditions, it is necessary to posit an alternative objective while at the same time insuring a competitive equilibrium solution will result.

Before looking at this alternative, let us define precisely what is meant by a competitive equilibrium solution in the current context.

Competitive Equilibrium Defined

An economic state is said to be in a competitive equilibrium if the following conditions are met:

1. Market equilibrium condition where there is homogeneity and uniqueness of the market demand price ρ_{1t}, the

market supply price ρ_{2t}, and the quasi-rent ρ_t^θ for each t and θ and no excess demand or excess supply possibility:

$$y_t - x_t \le 0 \qquad \rho_{1t}(y_t - x_t) = 0$$

$$x_t - \sum_{\theta=1}^{T} x_t^\theta \le 0 \qquad \rho_{2t}\left(x_t - \sum_{\theta=1}^{T} x_t^\theta\right) = 0$$

$$x_t^\theta \le W_\theta \qquad \rho_t^\theta\,(x_t^\theta - W_\theta) = 0 \text{ for all t and } \theta.$$

2. Optimum consumption equilibrium condition:

$$\rho_{1t} - f_t(y_t) \ge 0 \qquad y_t[\rho_{1t} - f_t(y_t)] = 0, \qquad t_t \ge 0.$$

3. Optimum production condition:

$$\rho_{2t} - c_t^\theta - \rho_t^\theta \le 0 \qquad x_t^\theta(\rho_{2t} - c_t^\theta - \rho_t^\theta) = 0, \qquad x_t^\theta \ge 0.$$

4. Optimum investment condition:

$$\sum_{t' \ge t} \sigma^{t'-t}\rho_{t'}^\theta - \xi_t \le 0 \qquad W_\theta\left(\sum_{t' \ge t} \sigma^{t'-t}\rho_{t'}^\theta - \xi_t\right) = 0, \qquad W_\theta \ge 0.$$

5. Price equilibrium:

$$\rho_{1t} - \rho_{2t} \le 0 \qquad x_t\,(\rho_{1t} - \rho_{2t}) = 0, \qquad x_t > 0.$$

At issue is the formulation of the problem so that these conditions are met. The results will yield the sought after competitive equilibrium conditions for peak load pricing.

AN ALTERNATIVE APPROACH TO MARGINAL COST PRICING WITH JOINT COSTS

An alternative objective function with considerable intuitive appeal that does not possess the limitations inherent in the consumer's surplus expression (7.2) is net revenue. Net revenue is the present value of total revenue less total cost

$$NR = \sum_{t=1}^{T} \sigma^{t-1}\left[y_t f_t(y_t) - \sum_{\theta=1}^{t} c_t^\theta\, x_t^\theta - \xi_t\, W_t\right]. \qquad (7.19)$$

The net revenue maximum problem is formulated as Problem 1: Find $\Psi(y, x, X, W, \rho)$ that maximizes the net revenue function (7.19) subject to

1. $f_t(y_t) - \rho_{1t} \leq 0$
2. $\rho_{2t} - c_t^\theta - \rho_t^\theta \leq 0$
3. $\rho_{1t} - \rho_{2t} \leq 0$
4. $\Sigma_{t' \geq t} \sigma^{t'-t} \rho_{t'}^\theta - \xi_t \leq 0$
5. $y_t - x_t \leq 0$
6. $x_t - \Sigma_{\theta=1}^T x_t^\theta \leq 0$
7. $x_t^\theta \leq W_\theta$
8. $y_t \geq 0,\ x_t^\theta \geq 0,\ x_t \geq 0,\ W_\theta \geq 0,\ \rho_{1t} \geq 0,\ \rho_{2t} \geq 0$, and $\rho_t^\theta \geq 0$ for all θ and t, and

where
$$y = \{y_t\};$$
$$x = \{x_t^\theta\};$$
$$X = \{x_t\};$$
$$W = \{W_\theta\};$$
$$\rho = \{\rho_{1t}, \rho_{2t}, \text{ and } \rho_t^\theta\}$$

This problem does not possess the nice property that the feasibility set is necessarily nonempty due to the first two constraint sets, (1) and (2). Thus, the only proof given here is that if a solution exists for this problem, the solution satisfies the competitive equilibrium stated above. For the Lagrangian,

$$\begin{aligned}\phi(y, x, X, W, \rho, \eta, P) = &\sum_{t=1}^{T} \sigma^{t-1} \Bigg[y_t f_t(y_t) - \sum_{\theta=1}^{T} c_t^\theta x_t^\theta - \xi_t W_t \\ &+ \sum_{t=1}^{T} \sigma^{t-1} \Bigg[\eta_{1t}(\rho_{1t} - f_t(y_t)) + \eta_{2t}(\rho_{2t} - \rho_{1t}) \\ &+ \sum_{\theta=1}^{T} \eta_{\theta t}(c_t^\theta + \rho_t^\theta - \rho_{2t}) \\ &+ \sum_{\theta=1}^{T} \eta_t^\theta \left(\xi_t - \sum_{t' \geq t} \sigma^{t'-t} \rho_{t'}^\theta \right) \Bigg] \\ &+ \sum_{t=1}^{T} \sigma^{t-1} \Bigg[P_{1t}(x_t - y_t) + P_{2t} \left(\sum_{\theta=1}^{T} x_t^\theta - x_t \right) \\ &+ \sum_{\theta=1}^{T} P_t^\theta(W_\theta - x_t^\theta) \Bigg], \end{aligned} \tag{7.20}$$

where η is the set of all η_{1t}, η_{2t}, $\eta_{\theta t}$, and η_t^θ and P is the set of all P_{1t}, P_{2t}, and P_t.

Providing the demand curves are downward sloping, the revenue function (7.19) is concave and the Kuhn-Tucker conditions will give the necessary and sufficient conditions for an optimum. After elimination of the discount factor, they are

$$y_t \le x_t \qquad P_{1t} \ge 0 \tag{7.21}$$

$$x_t \le \sum_{\theta=1}^{T} x_t^\theta \qquad P_{2t} \ge 0 \tag{7.22}$$

$$x_t^\theta \le W_\theta \qquad P_t^\theta \ge 0 \tag{7.23}$$

$$P_{1t} \le P_{2t} \qquad x_t > 0 \tag{7.24}$$

$$f_t(y_t) + y_t f_t'(y_t) - \eta_{1t} f_t'(y_t) \le P_{1t} \qquad y_t \ge 0 \tag{7.25}$$

$$P_{2t} \le c_t^\theta + P_t^\theta \qquad x_t^\theta \ge 0 \tag{7.26}$$

$$\sum_{t' \ge t} \sigma^{t'-t} P_{t'}^\theta \le \xi_t \qquad W_t \ge 0 \tag{7.27}$$

$$f_t(y_t) \le \rho_{1t} \qquad \eta_{1t} \ge 0 \tag{7.28}$$

$$\rho_{1t} \le \rho_{2t} \qquad \eta_{2t} \ge 0 \tag{7.29}$$

$$\rho_{2t} \le c_t^\theta + \rho_t^\theta \qquad \eta_{\theta t} \ge 0 \tag{7.30}$$

$$\sum_{t' \ge t} \sigma^{t'-t} \rho_{t'}^\theta \le \xi_t \qquad \eta_t^\theta \ge 0. \tag{7.31}$$

Conditions (7.21) through (7.27) are exactly the same as conditions (7.8) through (7.14) of the preceding section with the exception of condition (7.25). The interpretation of the conditions is identical. Conditions (7.28) through (7.31) are just those necessary to provide for optimum consumption, price equilibrium, optimum production, and optimum investment.

It is interesting to note that the objective function (7.19) is nonpositive as long as the variables are subject to the constraint set 1 through 8 found following the statement of Problem 1.

That is,

$$
\begin{aligned}
NR &= \sum_{t=1}^{T} \sigma^{t-1}\left[y_t f_t(y_t) - \sum_{\theta=1}^{T} c_t^\theta x_t^\theta - \xi_t W_t\right] \\
&\leq \sum_{t=1}^{T} \sigma^{t-1}\left(\sum_{\theta=1}^{T} x_t^\theta \rho_{1t} - \sum_{\theta=1}^{T} c_t^\theta x_t^\theta - \sum_{\theta=1}^{T} x_t^\theta \rho_t^\theta\right) \\
&= \sum_{t=1}^{T} \sigma^{t-1}\left[\sum_{\theta=1}^{T} x_t^\theta \rho_{1t} - \sum_{\theta=1}^{T}(c_t^\theta + \rho_t^\theta) x_t^\theta\right] \\
&\leq \sum_{t=1}^{T} \sigma^{t-1}\left[\sum_{\theta=1}^{T}(\rho_{1t} - \rho_{2t}) x_t^\theta\right] \\
&= \sum_{t=1}^{T} \sigma^{t-1}(\rho_{1t} - \rho_{2t})\, x_t \leq 0.
\end{aligned}
\tag{7.32}
$$

The first inequality is obtained from 1, and 4 to 7. The second inequality is obtained from 2. The last inequality is obtained from 3. The implications of this nonpositiveness of the objective function is that if a solution exists for the problem, then the maximum value of the objective function must be zero.

The dual of Problem 1 can be specified as Problem 2: Find (η, P) that minimizes $\phi(y, x, X, W, \rho, \eta, P)$ as given in Eq. (7.20).

Write the feasibility sets of Problem 1 and Problem 2 as R and S, respectively. Then we have the result

$$\max_{R} \Psi(y, x, X, W, \rho) = \min_{S} \phi(y, x, X, W, \rho, \eta, P) \tag{7.33}$$

if a solution exists for either of the two problems.[7]

However, since

$$\underset{\text{on R}}{\Psi(y, x, X, W, \rho) \leq 0} \tag{7.34}$$

and relation (7.33) holds, we get

$$\underset{\text{on R}}{\Psi(y, x, X, W, \rho)} \leq 0 \leq \underset{\text{on S}}{\phi(y, x, X, W, \rho, \eta, P)}. \tag{7.35}$$

Further, if $(\bar{y}, \bar{x}, \bar{X}, \bar{W}, \bar{\rho})$ solves Problem 1, then there exists a $(\bar{\eta}, \bar{P})$ such that

$$\Psi(\bar{y}, \bar{x}, \bar{X}, \bar{W}, \bar{\rho}) = \phi(\bar{y}, \bar{x}, \bar{X}, \bar{W}, \bar{\rho}, \bar{\eta}, \bar{P}) \tag{7.36}$$

which, due to Eq. (7.35), reduces to

$$\Psi(\bar{y}, \bar{x}, \bar{X}, \bar{W}, \bar{\rho}) = \phi(\bar{y}, \bar{x}, \bar{X}, \bar{W}, \bar{\rho}, \bar{\eta}, \bar{P}) = 0. \tag{7.37}$$

Therefore, if we assume that $(\bar{y}, \bar{x}, \bar{X}, \bar{W}, \bar{\rho})$ is a solution for Problem 1, then

$$\Psi(\bar{y}, \bar{x}, \bar{X}, \bar{W}, \bar{\rho}) = 0 \tag{7.38}$$

follows immediately.

By making use of the primal-dual method,[8] we can conclude that the dual solution set for Problem 2, consisting of $(\bar{\eta}, \bar{\rho})$, is exactly equal to the primal solution set consisting of $(\bar{y}, \bar{x}, \bar{X}, \bar{W}, \bar{\rho})$. That is, the solution set $(\bar{\eta}, \bar{\rho})$ is an eact replica of $(\bar{y}, \bar{x}, \bar{X}, \bar{W}, \bar{\rho})$.

Given this extremely interesting and simplifying property of the solution set, it is easy to justify the statement that the solution $(\bar{y}, \bar{x}, \bar{X}, \bar{W}, \bar{\rho})$ satisfies the conditions stipulated for a competitive equilibrium as defined above.

Thus, it has been proved that if the net revenue maximum problem yields a solution, the solution is a competitive price equilibrium solution, and the operating criteria are identical to those under the welfare-maximization approach involving consumer's surplus in the objective function.

CONCLUSION

If we adopt net revenue as the appropriate definition of social welfare to be maximized, the solution, if it exists, will yield a competitive equilibrium. This approach, though more demanding computationally, allows us to circumvent the problems associated with the maximization of an expression involving consumer's surplus.

Further, the net-revenue-maximization problem is a more general and pragmatic framework that when solved will attain an equilibrium for not only the nonintegrable case but the case where the integrability conditions are assumed to hold as well. It should be emphasized that in this formulation, a tangible objective such as profit is used rather than an intangible objective such as consumer's surplus.

NOTES AND REFERENCES

1. H. Hotelling, "The General Welfare in Relation to Problems of Taxation and Railway and Utility Rates." *Econometrica 6:* 242–269, 1938.
2. See I. Pressman, "A Mathematical Formulation of the Peak-Load Pricing Problem." *The Bell Journal of Economics and Management Science 1:* 304–326, 1970.
3. L. J. Lau, "Integrability of Consumer Preferences," processed, 1975.
4. This is the point of departure in the peak-load pricing formulations.
5. Lau, op. cit.
6. R. Turvey, "Marginal Cost." *The Economic Journal 79:* 282–299, 1969.
7. D. G. Luenberger, *Optimization by Vector Space Methods.* New York: John Wiley and Sons, Inc., 1969, pp. 223–225.
8. Ibid., pp. 299.

Chapter VIII

The Impact of Intertemporal Demand Dependencies on the Optimal Pricing of Public Utility Service

INTRODUCTION

In a previous chapter (Chapter II), the focus was on the pricing of public utility service when consumers and producers are spatially diffuse and when net social payoff maximization is the objective. One of the assumptions used in the model developed in that chapter is that demands are temporally independent. For longer term considerations where the time period of focus is seasons or years this does not seem to be an unwarranted assumption. Over a shorter horizon (daily or weekly), however, this does not appear to be the case. In fact, some recent empirical work on electric utilities (e.g., Atkinson[1]) shows that demands in different periods of the day are clearly interrelated. What is not clear is whether those demands are substitutes or complements. To the extent it is feasible for consumers to postpone the consumption of a service, for example, they are substitutes. On the other hand, factors exist which tend to make demands complements. For example, the existence of inexpensive off-peak charges for phone calls may increase the demand for peak phone calls. Many households which are induced to have the telephone installed because of low off-peak rates may in turn use the phone during the peak period which they otherwise would not have done had no phone been present in the home. Thus, the demand for phone calls in different periods, in the aggregate, might be substitutes or complements, and whether they are one or the other is an empirical question.

Given these considerations, it is imperative to examine the implications for the situation in which temporal demands are substitutes and for the situations in which they are complements. This is the objective here. The model is developed with specific reference to electrical energy, but that does not preclude the possibility of adapting it to consider the markets for public utilities in subsequent applications. The general conclusions are uniformly applicable.

ORIENTATION

As a basis for the specification, the problem of equilibrium among spatially and temporally separated markets is couched in terms of the underlying demand and supply relations and is defined as the sum of the areas under the demand functions less the sum of the areas under the supply functions at posttrade equilibrium prices (i.e., after electrical energy has been generated and sold to consumers) minus the sum of the areas under the demand functions less the sum of the areas under the supply functions at pretrade prices minus the total transmission and distribution costs incurred. Because the sum of the areas under the demand functions less the sum of the areas under the supply functions at pretrade prices is constant, it may be omitted from the definition without altering the posttrade prices and allocation. Further, it is necessary to introduce delivery costs (transmission and distribution) to capture the spatial aspects of the problem.

ENVIRONMENT

Visualize an environment where there are many consumers of electrical energy and many generating plants each of which is spatially separated. To formulate the understanding and development of the model, the following definitions and notation are introduced.

Let $i = 1, 2, ..., N$ denote the consumers;

$j = 1, 2, ..., \theta$ denote the generating plants;[2]

$t,\tau = 1, 2, ..., T$ denote the discrete time periods of equal length;

y_{ijt} = quantity of electrical energy demanded by consumer i from plant j in period t;

x_{jit} = quantity of electrical energy supplied by plant j to consumer i in period t;

x_{jt} = quantity of electrical energy generated by plant j in period t;

I_{jt} = investment in generating plant j that will be available for operation in period t;

$\hat{I}_{jt}$ = maximum possible investment in generating plant j in period t;

K_{j1} = generating capacity of plant j in period 1;

β_{jt} = capital cost for an additional unit of generating capacity for plant j in period t (this is assumed to be constant as is customary in the peak load pricing literaure[3]);

d_{jit} = delivery cost of electrical energy generated by plant j and distributed to consumer i in period t;

r = rate of interest.

Relying on the assumption that the demand functions of each consumer for each time period are known with certainty or are available in the certainty equivalence sense and further that the demand in any period is dependent on the price in that period and in other periods, the demand functions are given in the form

$$P_{ijt} = g_{ijt}(y_{ij1}, y_{ij2}, ..., y_{ijT}), \tag{8.1}$$

where P_{ijt} is the price of electrical energy to consumer i from plant j in period t.

Similarly, assume the operating cost functions (including fuel costs) are known with certainty or are available in the certainty equivalence sense and that operating costs are temporally independent. The operating cost functions are given by

$$\Omega_{jt} = h_{jt}(x_{jt}), \tag{8.2}$$

where Ω_{jt} is the marginal cost of generation per kilowatt-hour on plant j in period t.

The search for optimum demands, prices, and operating schedules is subject to a number of constraints:

1. For each plant in each time period, the total quantity of electrical energy generated by a plant must be equal to the quantity demanded by all consumers from that plant:

$$y_{jt} = \sum_{i} x_{jit}, \tag{8.3}$$

where the total quantity of electrical energy demanded from plant j is the sum of the quantities by all consumers ($y_{jt} = \Sigma_i y_{ijt}$).

2. For each plant and each time period, total generation of electrical energy is equal to the quantity supplied by that plant to all consumers:

$$\sum_{i} x_{jit} = x_{jt}. \tag{8.4}$$

3. For each plant and each time period, total generation is equal to the generation from that plant existing in the initial period plus the generation from new capacity added in the first and subsequent periods:

$$x_{jt} = K_{j1} + \sum_{\tau=1}^{t} I_{j\tau}. \tag{8.5}$$

There is a temptation to include a term to account for the rate of decline in output over time due to "age." However, since it is not significant for well-maintained generating plants, the term is excluded. Further, if capacity is not added in period t or the plant does not exist in the intial period, I_{jt} or K_{j1} will be appropriately zero.

4. For each region, investment in generating capacity of a plant is constrained by physical, institutional, and technological limitations:

$$I_{jt} \leq \hat{I}_{jt}. \tag{8.6}$$

For example, it is well recognized that there is a maximum feasible expansion in, say, nuclear power development considering the constraints imposed by such things as licensing, development of additional uranium supplies, technical and construction manpower limitations, and difficulties with new and extrapolated equipment.

5. For each plant, consumer, and time period there is a maximum transmission of electrical energy:

$$x_{jit} \leq \hat{x}_{jit}, \tag{8.7}$$

where $\hat{x}_{jit}$ denotes the maximum technologically feasible transmission.

In analyzing this problem, it is also necessary to expand the analysis beyond the previous scope. In particular, public utilities are regulated monopolies rather than extensions of the government whose objective it is to provide a social welfare service. Hence, if social welfare maximization is to serve as the objective, it must be subject to a revenue constraint. Thus,

$$\sum_i \sum_j P_{ijt} y_{ijt} - \sum_j \Omega_{jt}(x_{jt}) - \sum_i \sum_j d_{jit} x_{jit} = R_t, \tag{8.8}$$

where R_t represents a regulatory constraint that fixes a profit maximum in a specific period.

A MODEL OF PEAK-LOAD PRICING WITH INTERDEPENDENT DEMANDS

It is now possible to form the Hotelling-type[4] quasi-welfare function W for the peak-load pricing model as follows:

$$W = \sum_t \sigma^{t-1} \left[\sum_i \sum_j \int g_{ijt}(y_{ij1}, y_{ij2}, \ldots, y_{ijT})\, dy_{ijt} - \sum_j \int h_{jt}(x_{jt})\, dx_{jt} - \sum_j \beta_{jt} I_{jt} - \sum_i \sum_j d_{jit} x_{jit} \right], \tag{8.9}$$

where $\sigma^{t-1} = \dfrac{1}{(1+r)^{t-1}}$.

Providing the demand functions are downward sloping, the objective function is concave and the Kuhn-Tucker conditions will give the necessary and sufficient conditions for a competitive solution. Associate the dual variables $\sigma^{t-1}\rho_{1jt}$, $\sigma^{t-1}\rho_{2jt}$, $\sigma^{t-1}\rho_{3jt}$, $\sigma^{t-1}\rho_{4jt}$, $\sigma^{t-1}\rho_{tji}$, and $\sigma^{t-1}\rho_{6t}$ with constraints (8.3) through (8.8). Multiplying through by σ^{t-1} where appropriate, the Kuhn-Tucker conditions are

$$y_{jt} \leq \sum_i x_{jit} \qquad \rho_{1jt} \geq 0 \tag{8.10}$$

$$\sum_i x_{jit} \leq x_{jt} \qquad \rho_{2jt} \geq 0 \quad (8.11)$$

$$x_{jt} \leq K_{j1} + \sum_{\tau=1}^{t} I_{j\tau} \qquad \rho_{3jt} \geq 0 \quad (8.12)$$

$$I_{jt} \leq \hat{I}_{jt} \qquad \rho_{4jt} \geq 0 \quad (8.13)$$

$$X_{jit} \leq \hat{X}_{jit} \qquad \rho_{5jit} \geq 0 \quad (8.14)$$

$$\sum_i \sum_j P_{ijt} y_{ijt} - \sum_j h_{jt}(X_{it}) - \sum_i \sum_j d_{jit} X_{jit} \leq R_t \qquad \rho_{6t} \geq 0 \quad (8.15)$$

$$P_{ijt} \leq \rho_{ijt} - \rho_{6jt}\left(P_{ijt} + \sum_i \sum_j y_{ijt} \frac{\partial P_{ijt}}{\partial y_{ijt}}\right) \qquad y_{ijt} \geq 0 \quad (8.16)$$

$$\rho_{ijt} \leq \gamma_{jit} + \rho_{2jt} + \rho_{5jit} + \rho_{6it} d_{jit} \qquad x_{jit} \geq 0 \quad (8.17)$$

$$\rho_{2jt} \leq \frac{\partial \Omega_{jt}}{\partial x_{jt}} + \rho_{3jt} + \rho_{6t} \frac{\partial \Omega_{jt}}{\partial x_{jt}} \qquad x_{jt} \geq 0 \quad (8.18)$$

$$\sum_{t' \geq t} \sigma^{t'-t} \rho_{3jt} \leq \beta_{jt} + \rho_{4jt} \qquad I_{jt} \geq 0 \quad (8.19)$$

ρ_{3jt} is interpreted as the quasi-rent of plant j in period t and, if that plant is utilized, is equal to the supply price minus marginal operating cost[5] adjusted for the impact of the profit constraint. Thus, if

$$x_{jt} > 0, \qquad \text{then } \rho_{3jt} = \rho_{2jt} - (1 + \rho_{6t})MC_{jt}. \quad (8.20)$$

Suppose, in addition, $y_{ijt} > 0$ and $0 < x_{jit} < \hat{x}_{jit}$. To minimize total cost, production will be scheduled on equipment in increasing order of marginal operating cost and delivery cost. Therefore, the price to a consumer in period t equals the delivery cost plus marginal operating cost on the least-efficient plant, denoted by j*, being used to generate electrical energy adjusted for the effect of the profit constraint (this will be more fully explored below). Thus, if

$$0 < x_{j^*t} < K_{j^*1} + \sum_{\tau=1}^{t} I_{j^*\tau},$$

then

$$P_{ij^*t} = \gamma_{j^*it} + MC_{j^*t} + \frac{\rho_{6t}}{1 + \rho_{6t}}\left(\sum_i \sum_j y_{ijt} \frac{\partial P_{ijt}}{\partial y_{ijt}}\right). \tag{8.21}$$

The quasi-rent of any plant j in use is equal to the difference between its marginal operating cost (adjusted) plus delivery cost and these costs accounted for by the least-efficient plant. Thus, if

$$x_{jt} > 0, \qquad \text{then } \rho_{3jt} = (1 + \rho_{6t})MC_{j^*t} + d_{j^*it} - [(1 + \rho_{6jt})MC_{jt} + \gamma_{jit} + \rho_{5jit}] \tag{8.22}$$

Note that it is possible to use a plant to generate electrical energy that does not have the lowest operating cost. If the delivery cost is sufficiently large, then it might be optimal to use a plant with a higher operating cost while shutting down a more efficient one.

Additions to capacity are undertaken on the basis of a least-cost criterion. New capacity (either an additional plant or an expansion of an existing plant) should be added in any period up to the point where the discounted sum of its quasi-rents equals the purchase price plus the marginal value of a particular plant addition (or quasi-rent arising because the capacity expansion is limited). Thus, if

$$I_{jt} > 0, \qquad \text{then } \sum_{t' \geq t} \sigma^{t'-t} \rho_{3jt} = \beta_{jt} + \rho_{4jt}. \tag{8.23}$$

The quasi-rent of a plant in any period can be regarded as that part of the supply price set aside to cover depreciation and interest on capital. This is what Turvey calls *amortization.*[6] If new capacity is added in any period, and if the maximum capacity addition is not reached, demand price in that period is equal to operating cost plus amortization on the new plant plus delivery cost plus an adjustment. Thus, denoting the new plant capacity by n, if

$$x_{nt} > 0 \qquad y_{int} > 0,$$

then

$$P_{int} = \gamma_{nit} + MC_{nt} + \rho_{3nt} + \frac{\rho_{6t}}{1 + \rho_{6t}}\left(\sum_i \sum_n y_{int} \frac{\partial P_{int}}{\partial y_{int}}\right). \tag{8.24}$$

A plant m should begin to be retired when its operating cost rises above the level of $MC_{nt} + \rho_{3nt}$ (given the delivery costs are equal). Thus, if

$$MC_{mt} < MC_{nt} + \rho_{3nt}, \qquad \text{then} \quad X_{mt} = 0. \tag{8.25}$$

Equation (8.23) can be interpreted to mean that the present value of amortization equals the purchase price of new capacity plus the quasi-rent of the capacity limitation. Therefore, the amount set aside for amortization varies from period to period, depending on demand and perhaps is equal to zero in some periods. With demand varying, a constant proportion of capacity cost each period should not necessarily be recouped. Rather, price should be set to just fully utilize capacity (conditional upon price not being below marginal production cost), and capacity should be selected so that over the life of the plant, capacity cost is just recouped.

In Chapter II it was demonstrated that if the demands are independent between periods, then the price in any particular period will just equal marginal operating cost plus delivery cost plus quasi-rent. When demands are temporally interdependent, the situation is different, as outlined in Eqs. (8.17) and (8.24). The value of interest is that which occurs in parentheses in the last term of each of these relations with the implication being that prices in off-peak periods, for example (i.e., when no new capacity is being added), will necessarily be affected by prices in the peak periods, and vice versa, is demonstrated in what follows.

For convenience of exposition consider a two-period case (a peak period and an off-peak period), realizing that the conclusions apply equally well to the general case of more than two periods. Denoting the off-peak period by 1 and the peak period by 2, the price in period 2 should always be higher than that of period 1, given the outputs in the two periods are equal. Further, assume there is only a single consumer (allowing for the deletion of subscript i) and a single generating plant (allowing for the deletion of subscript j) and no delivery cost.

Thus, for the two-period case,

$$P_1 = MC_1 + \frac{\rho_{61}}{1 + \rho_{61}} \left(y_1 \frac{\partial P_1}{\partial y_1} + y_2 \frac{\partial P_2}{\partial y_1} \right) \tag{8.26}$$

$$P_2 = MC_2 + \rho_{32} + \frac{\rho_{62}}{1 + \rho_{62}}\left(y_2 \frac{\partial P_2}{\partial y_2} + y_1 \frac{\partial P_1}{\partial y_2}\right). \tag{8.27}$$

Since the price and quantity in period t are inversely related, $\partial P_t/\partial y_t < 0$.

In so far as demands in different periods are imperfect substitutes, it is to be expected that a given change in the quantity supplied in any given period t will reduce the price in that period by a greater amount than it will reduce the price in another period t′ so that it is expected

$$\left|\frac{\partial P_t}{\partial y_t}\right| > \left|\frac{\partial P_{t'}}{\partial y_{t'}}\right|, \qquad t \neq t'.$$

If the demands in the two periods are complements, then an increase in the quantity supplied in period t increases the price that consumers are prepared to pay for a given quantity in the other period t′, $\partial P_t/\partial y_t > 0$, but it is still expected that the increase in the price in period t is less than the fall in the price in period t′, that is,

$$\left|\frac{\partial P_t}{\partial y_t}\right| > \frac{\partial P_{t'}}{\partial y_t} > 0.$$

The consequence of this is that in a shifting-peak solution in which $y_1 = y_2$, $MC_t < P_t$, $t = 1, 2$ even if $\partial P_{t'}/\partial y_t > 0$. In a firm (stationary) peak solution, however, in which $y_1 < y_2$, $MC_2 < P_2$ but MC_1 is no longer less than P_1. It is feasible for MC_1 to be greater than or equal to P_1. In other words, if the demands in the peak and off-peak periods are complements and if off-peak capacity is underutilized, then it is possible for marginal cost to exceed price in the off-peak period but not in the peak period.

In terms of elasticities,[7] Eqs. (8.28) and (8.29) are

$$P_1 = \frac{1}{\Delta_1}\left(MC_1 + \frac{\xi_1 \varepsilon_{12}(MC_2 + \rho_{32})}{1 - \xi_2}\right) \tag{8.28}$$

$$P_2 = \frac{1}{\Delta_2}\left(MC_2 + \rho_{32} + \frac{\xi_2 \varepsilon_{21} MC_1}{1 - \xi_1}\right) \tag{8.29}$$

where $\xi_1 = \dfrac{\rho_{61}}{1 + \rho_{61}}$

$$\xi_2 = \frac{\rho_{62}}{1 + \rho_{62}}$$

$$\Delta_1 = \frac{1 - \xi_1 - \xi_2 + \xi_1\xi_2 (1 - \varepsilon_{12}\varepsilon_{21})}{1 - \xi_2}$$

$$\Delta_2 = \frac{1 - \xi_1 - \xi_2 + \xi_1\xi_2 (1 - \varepsilon_{12}\varepsilon_{21})}{1 - \xi_1}$$

and

$$\varepsilon_{tt'} = \frac{y_t}{P_{t'}} \frac{\partial P_{t'}}{\partial_{y_t}} \begin{cases} < 0 & \text{for } t = t' \text{ or for } t \neq t' \text{ and demands are substitutes} \\ > 0 & \text{for } t \neq t' \text{ and demands are complements} \\ = 0 & \text{for } t \neq t' \text{ and demands are independent} \\ & t, t' = 1, 2. \end{cases}$$

What relations (8.28) and (8.29) show is that price in any period is a weighted average of the marginal cost in both periods.

Implications From the Model

The formulation of the problem in the spatial dimension as well as the temporal dimension has permitted the handling of many problems concerned with investment in generating capacity as well as the problems involved with price adjustment and allocation over time.

The general principles of optimal pricing can be summarized as follows:

1. Set prices by time of day (or seasons of the year) in accordance with the pattern of demand. This means that any consumer in a particular hour be treated the same regardless of how much he consumes. Further, prices in any period depend on the marginal operating costs and capital costs in all periods.
2. Vary prices spatially depending upon how far the consumer is from the generating plant.
3. Charge the consumer enough to cover delivery cost. This

means that it is acceptable to charge residential and industrial consumers different prices because the delivery costs for the two classes are different.

It is worthwhile to more fully investigate the price and output effects when demands are interdependent. An adjustment to the profit constraint will be used as the medium through which the effects are investigated. Assume a reduction in the level of maximum profit. This will in turn result in an increase in the value of ρ_{6t}. Whether this will increase or decrease the price and consequently output is dependent upon whether the demands between periods are complements or substitutes. In the case of complementarity, $\varepsilon_{tt'} < 0$, and the price will fall with a consequent increase in demand. For the situation when the demands are substitutes, $\varepsilon_{tt'} > 0$ resulting in an increase in price and quantity demanded.

SUMMARY

The principal issue addressed in this chapter was the price profile for a regulated public utility where demand and supply vary spatially and temporally, and where demands are temporally interdependent. No simple cost-based solution proves possible. Price is determined as a weighted average of marginal operating costs in all periods, capital costs in all periods, and delivery costs.

After going through the preceding discussion, the obvious question arising is whether, in the case of electrical energy, the demands between periods are complementary. This being an empirical question, it is necessary to reference some of the analysis of the peak-load pricing experiments currently being funded in part by the Department of Energy. The results from these experiments do indicate that demands are complementary between periods. For example, Lau and Lillard[8] find a cross-price elasticity between the off-peak and peak periods of −.35 for the households analyzed in the Arizona experiment. Others have found analogous results using different approaches and experiments (see EPRI[9]). The substance of this is that the discussion of complementarity and substitutability is not moot.

NOTES AND REFERENCES

1. S. E. Atkinson, "A Preliminary Analysis of FEA's Time-of-Day Electricity Pricing Experiments." *Journal of Econometrics,* forthcoming.
2. It is assumed that two plants in close physical proximity are distinct entities.
3. See I. Pressman, "A Mathematical Formulation of the Peak-Load Pricing Problem." *The Bell Journal of Economics and Management Science 1:* 304–326, 1970.
4. H. Hotelling, "The General Welfare in Relation to Problems of Taxation and of Railway and Utility Rates." *Econometrica 6:* 242–269, 1938.
5. Marginal operating cost on plant j in period t, MC_{jt}, is equal to $MC_{jt} = \partial\Omega_{jt}/\partial x_{jt}$.
6. R. Turvey and D. Anderson, *Electricity Economics.* Baltimore, Md.: The Johns Hopkins University Press, 1977.
7. Note that these elasticities are not conventional elasticities but are elasticities evaluated under the assumption that all prices are allowed to change so as to maintain all other quantities constant.
8. L. J. Lau, and L. A. Lillard, "A Random Response Model of the Demand for Electricity by Time-of-Day." In A. Lawrence (ed.), *Proceedings of a Workshop on Modelling and Analysis of Electricity by Time-of-Day.* Palo Alto, Calif.: Electric Power Research Institute, 1978.
9. Electric Power Research Institute, *Proceedings of a Workshop on Modelling and Analysis of Electricity by Time-of-Day.* Palo Alto, Calif.: Electric Power Research Institute, June 1978.

Chapter IX

The Pricing of Public Utility Service with Stochastic Demands Subject to Regulatory Constraint

INTRODUCTION

As noted frequently in the preceding pages, recent years have seen a renewed interest in the question of the optimal pricing of public utility service. In the case of the electrical energy industry, the motivation for such interest has arisen because changes in the international and domestic energy arena have altered industry fundamentals upon which many of the past practices have rested. It is now imperative that the industry rethink its ways of operating to coincide with the new economic realities.

One area of probable change concerns present expectations for sharp increases in the electric utility industry's demand for capital. As a consequence of recent economic events, the utilities newly acquired higher cost of capital will encourage them to shift away from capital intensive forms of power generation (e.g., nuclear) toward less capital-intensive methods (e.g., fossil-fueled coal plants). If this is done for short-term financial, rather than sound economic reasons, future electric costs and, hence, prices may well turn out to be higher than they otherwise need to be. The most promising area for cost reduction seems to be that of generation expenditures. It is possible for electric utilities to reduce their construction budgets and relieve their near term financial problems through improved rationalization of the operating reliability criteria. This is the subject of what follows.

Background

Brown and Johnson[1] have shown that the optimal utility price under risk will be equal to marginal operating cost and hence will always be smaller than its counterpart in the riskless model of traditional theory. This conclusion is based on the implicit assumption that in the eventuality of demand exceeding capacity, there is no social cost associated with the rationing of output among consumers. In commenting on this, Turvey[2] points out that rationing of output can cause serious problems for consumers of public utility services—in particular, electrical energy—so that price is usually set high enough to keep the risk of failure down to a minimum level. That is, a de facto price is set in excess of operating cost. Turvey unfortunately does not provide a formal analysis deriving the implications of his contention. Had this been done, the analysis would most likely have shown that the optimal price in the case of risk will not differ significantly from the optimal price in the riskless situation.

Given these considerations, this study endeavors to improve on previous results and comments. It has two unique aspects. The first is the explicit inclusion of a rationing constraint analogous to that introduced by Visscher.[3] The second is that the results are made conformable to the earlier work of Chapters II, IV, and VI.

A MODEL OF PRICING WITH STOCHASTIC DEMAND

Once again it is necessary to slightly alter the notation and problem formulation from that previously used to allow the determination of an optimal price to be mathematically tractable. Thus, considerations of capacity expansion are included as part of generation and not separately as before. Net social welfare maximization continues to be the objective.

Assume that an economy exists where the demand for electrical energy can be met by many different generating plants. To formulate the understanding and development of the model, the following definitions and notation are introduced.

Let j = generating plants;
t = discrete time periods;
y_t = quantity of electrical energy demanded in period t;[4]
$\overline{X}_{jt}$ = capacity output of plant j in period t;
d_{jt} = delivery cost (transmission and distribution costs) from plant j in period t (assumed to be equal for all consumers);
b_{jt} = cost of capital for an additional unit of generating capacity for plant j in period t;
a_{jt} = operating cost (including fuel cost) for plant j in period t, and
r = rate of interest.

Assume, as do Brown and Johnson, that each plant manager knows the aggregate demand function

$$y_t(P_t, u_t), \tag{9.1}$$

where u_t is a continuous random variable in period t. Further, it is assumed that the exact form of the continuous probability density function $f(u_t)$ is given. The following properties are attributable to $f(u_t)$.

$$\begin{aligned} F(Z) &= \int_{-\infty}^{\infty} f(u_t)\, du_t \\ &\int_{-\infty}^{\infty} u_t f(u_t)\, du_t = 0 \\ &\int_{-\infty}^{\infty} u_t^2 f(u_t)\, du_t < \infty, \end{aligned} \tag{9.2}$$

where F(Z) defines the probability of $u_t \leq z$. The second expression indicates that first moment (mean) is zero and the last expression denotes that the second moment is finite.

In the subsequent analysis, it will be assumed that the error term is additive. Thus, demand is given by

$$y_t = y_t\,(P_t) + u_t. \tag{9.3}$$

Given the price there will be a corresponding $y_t\,(P_t)$ to which will be added a random term. Consequently, for actual sales of electrical energy in period t,

$$Q_t = \begin{cases} y_t(P_t) + u_t & u_t \leq \sum_j \overline{X}_{jt} - y_t(P_t) \\ \\ \sum_j \overline{X}_{jt} & u_t > \sum_j \overline{X}_{jt} - y_t(P_t). \end{cases} \tag{9.4}$$

If actual demand is less than generating capacity, then the quantity demanded will be exactly equal to actual sales. If for the given price, however, a value of u_t should occur such that $y_t(P_t,\, u_t)$ is greater than capacity, actual sales cannot exceed capacity although demand potentially can.

Following closely the pattern established by the earlier riskless theory, the arguments of the Hotelling-type welfare function W to be maximized include the expected value of willingness to pay, the expected value of variable cost (including operating and maintenance cost and delivery cost), and the capacity cost, assumed to be known with certainty or available in the certainty equivalence sense.

Using the previously delineated notation, this translates into

$$W = \sum_t \sigma^{t-1} \Bigg[\int_0^{y_t(p_t)+u_t} \overline{P}_t(y_t - u_t)\, dy_t - \sum_j (a_{jt} + d_{jt}) y_t(P_t) - \sum_j b_{jt}\overline{X}_{jt} \Bigg] \tag{9.5}$$

where $\overline{P}_t$ is the inverse demand function possessing the necessary regularity properties (e.g., $\partial\overline{P}_t/\partial y_t < 0$) and $\sigma^{t-1} = 1/1(1 + r)^{t-1}$. The problem of interest is to maximize the expected value of W over the set of nonnegative prices and capacity. It is necessary to assume in doing this that the random variable u_t exists for all feasible price and capacity vectors.

The Kuhn-Tucker conditions for the saddle value problem (in this case of the welfare maximizer) are well known to be

$$\frac{\partial W}{\partial P_t} = P_t y_t'(P_t) F\left[\sum_j \overline{X}_{jt} - y_t(P_t)\right]$$

$$- (a_{jt} + d_{jt}) y_t'(P_t) F\left[\sum_j \overline{X}_{jt} - y_t(P_t)\right]$$

$$\leq 0 \qquad \text{for } P_t \geq 0 \tag{9.6}$$

and

$$\frac{\partial W}{\partial \overline{X}_{jt}} = \sum_t \int_{\Sigma_j \overline{X}_{jt} - y_t(P_t)}^{\infty} f(u_t)\left[\overline{P}\left(\sum \overline{X}_{jt} - u_t\right)\right.$$

$$\left. - (a_{jt} + d_{jt})\right] du_t - b_{jt}$$

$$\leq 0 \qquad \text{for } \overline{X}_{jt} \geq 0, \tag{9.7}$$

where, as before, f is the density function and F is the cumulative distribution function of the random variable u_t.

Note in passing that since $F(\hat{u}_t) = \Pr(u_t \leq \hat{u}_t)$ by the definition of a cumulative distribution function (Pr denotes probability)

$$F\left(\sum_j \overline{X}_{jt} - y\right) = \Pr\left(u_t \leq \sum \overline{X}_{jt} - y_t(P_t)\right)$$

$$= \Pr\left(y_t(P_t) + u_t \leq \sum \overline{X}_{jt}\right)$$

is simply the reliability in period t. If $P_t > 0$ and if reliability is nonzero, then from Eq. (9.6)

$$P_t = a_{jt} + d_{jt}, \tag{9.8}$$

where implicitly plant j is the last to be brought on line (i.e., the combined operating and delivery costs for this plant exceed those of all other plants). (See Chapter II.)

It is possible, however, that reliability [i.e., $F(\Sigma_j \overline{X}_{jt} - y_t(P_t))$] is zero so that deleting this expression in Eq. (9.6) is not justified. While the interpretation of the Kuhn-Tucker conditions in this case are not as transparent as before, they do have an economic meaning. Specifically, the marginal loss in consumer surplus and revenue in excess of variable cost in period t from not increasing capacity slightly is $\overline{P}(\Sigma_j \overline{X}_{jt} - u_t) - (a_{jt} + d_{jt})$ if capacity is exceeded and zero otherwise. Thus, relation (9.7) says set $\Sigma_j \overline{X}_{jt}$ just large enough so that marginal expected losses due to unmet demand are equal to marginal capacity cost b_{jt}. To do this when uncertainty is small or capacity cost large would generally require the peak price to be higher than $a_{jt} + d_{jt}$.

The Rationing Cost

For the integration of the objective function, Eq. (9.5), to accurately measure consumers' surplus, it is necessary to assume that in the event of the quantity demanded exceeding capacity, consumers will be ranked according to their willingness to pay. Unlike Brown and Johnson, the presumption is that this process is not costless. In the spirit of Sherman and Visscher[5] and Visscher,[6] in the event of scarcity, costs are incurred in insuring that consumers are rationed in accordance with their marginal willingness to pay. For a utility employing a two-part tariff, for example, negotiations might occur between the electric utility and its consumers whereby it agrees to pay in some sense (e.g., through a reduction in rates) those consumers who will be cut off in the event that the quantity demanded exceeds capacity. While the present analysis does not incorporate such a scheme, the contention is that there are costs in rationing according to the willingness to pay in the event of excess demand. Additionally, as the magnitude of excess demand increases, it is likely that the transactions costs from dealing with more consumers when viewed from the electric utility's perspective will increase. Consequently, the sum of such costs when the quantity demand exceeds capacity is

$$R = \sum_t \gamma_t \left[y_t(P_t) + u_t - \sum_j \overline{X}_{jt} \right], \qquad (9.9)$$

where γ_t is the rationing cost incurred whenever capacity is exceeded and wherever it is monotonically increasing, convex, and differentiable. Combining this cost with the previous objective function yields the new measure of welfare:

$$\Omega(W, \gamma) = W - \sum_t \gamma_t \left[y_t(P_t) + u_t - \sum_j \overline{X}_{jt} \right]. \tag{9.10}$$

Following the previous procedure, the expected value of Eq. (9.10) is maximized. The Kuhn-Tucker conditions are given as

$$\begin{aligned} \frac{\partial \Omega}{\partial P_t} &= P_t y_t'(P_t)\, F\left(\sum_j \overline{X}_{jt} - y_t(P_t)\right) \\ &\quad - (a_{jt} + d_{jt}) y_t'(P_t) F\left(\sum_j \overline{X}_{jt} - y_t(P_t)\right) \\ &\quad - \gamma_t \left(1 - F\left(\sum_j \overline{X}_{jt} - y_t(P_t)\right) y_t'(P_t)\right) \\ &\leq 0 \qquad \text{for } P_t \geq 0 \end{aligned} \tag{9.11}$$

$$\begin{aligned} \frac{\partial \Omega}{\partial \overline{X}_{jt}} &= \sum_t \int_{\Sigma_j \overline{X}_{jt} - y_t(Pt)}^{\infty} f(u_t) \left[\overline{P}_t \left(\sum_j \overline{X}_{jt} - u_t \right) - (a_{jt} + d_{jt}) \right] du_t \\ &\quad - b_{jt} + \gamma_t \left[1 - F\left(\sum_j \overline{X}_{jt} - y_t(P_t) \right) \right] \\ &\leq 0 \qquad \text{for } \overline{X}_{jt} \geq 0. \end{aligned} \tag{9.12}$$

When reliability is nonzero and $P_t > 0$ dividing through by $F(\Sigma_j \overline{X}_{jt} - y_t(P_t))$ yields

$$P_t = a_{jt} + d_{jt} + \frac{\gamma_t[1 - F(\Sigma_j \overline{X}_{jt} - y(P))]}{F(\Sigma_j \overline{X}_{jt} - yt(P_t))}, \tag{9.13}$$

where, again, implicitly plant j is the last to be brought on line. Thus, price is set equal to the sum of marginal operating, delivery, and rationing costs, but it is also a function of reliability. A determination of the optimal level of reliability is accomplished by using relation (9.12). This indicates that, for $\overline{X}_{jt} > 0$, the reserve margin $\Sigma_j \overline{X}_{jt} - y_t(P_t)$ should be set so the marginal cost of capacity equals the sum of the expected marginal rationing cost and the consumer's surplus losses. Now if the losses in consumer's surplus [the first term on the right-hand side of relation (9.10)] are approximately zero (as suggested by Brown and Johnson, p. 125), then the marginal cost of capacity is

$$b_{jt} = \gamma_t\left[1 - F\left(\sum_j \overline{X}_{jt} - y_t(P_t)\right)\right] \tag{9.14}$$

or

$$1 - F\left(\sum_j \overline{X}_{jt} - y_t(P_t)\right) = \frac{b_{jt}}{\gamma_t}. \tag{9.14a}$$

This says that the ratio of the marginal capacity cost (of, implicitly, the last plant brought on line) to the marginal rationing cost determines the optimal level of reliability. Further, combining this with relation (9.11), and assuming $P_t > 0$, then

$$P_t = a_{jt} + d_{jt} + \frac{b_{jt}}{(F(\Sigma_j \overline{X}_{jt} - y_t(P_t))}. \tag{9.15}$$

The implication is that if the error term has the characteristics previously attributed to it, Eq. (9.14a) defines the level of $\overline{X}_{jt}$ such that the probability of failure to meet demand (one minus the level of reliability) is less than a specified level for the optimally determined price.

Further, the level of reliability has a larger impact on price than is explicitly represented in Eq. (9.15). In particular, capacity expansion plans will be adjusted so that Eq. (9.14) is satisfied. This will necessarily yield a higher level of capacity the greater the desired level of reliability. Since capacity is installed and brought into use on the basis of merit ordering (i.e., in increasing order of cost), price will be set equal to this higher value. Thus, de facto, both are coincidentally determined. That is, if one is given the capacity cost (and hence the level of capacity), then the level of reliability and the price are determined. Alternatively, given the reliability level, both the capacity level and price are known.

Different Consumer Groups

To carry the preceding analysis one step farther, it would be useful (and more realistic) to consider the existence of individual consumers or consumer groups as in preceding chapters.

It is assumed that they have distinct demand functions given by

$$y_{it} = y_{it}(P_{it}) + u_{it}, \qquad i = 1, 2, \tag{9.16}$$

where the random variable possesses the previously delineated characteristics. (The general formulation can contain any number of consumers. To simplify the algebra, however, only two are assumed.)

When the quantity demanded exceeds capacity, rationing occurs. Of central importance when this occurs is how demand is apportioned among the different consumer groups. That is the subject of this section.

To simplify the characterization, assume that each group of consumers incurs a constant share of excess demand, ξ_i, i = 1, 2. This allows for a reformulation of the objective function as

$$\begin{aligned}\Psi = \sum_t \sigma^{t-1}\Bigg(&\int_0^{y_{it}(P_{it})+u_{it}} \overline{P}_{it}(y_{it} - u_{it})\, dy_{it} \\ &- \sum_i \sum_j (a_{jt} + d_{jt}) y_{it}(P_{it}) - \sum b_{jt}\overline{X}_{jt} \\ &- \sum_i \gamma_{it}\xi_i \left\{\sum_i [y_{it}(P_{it}) + u_{it}] - \sum_j \overline{X}_{jt}\right\}\Bigg),\end{aligned} \tag{9.17}$$

where $\xi_i(\Sigma\, y_{it} + u_{it} - \Sigma_j\, \overline{X}_{jt})$ is just the share of excess demand attributable to consumer group i, and where, as before, $\overline{P}_{it}$ is the inverse demand function with the requisite properties.

Observe that in specifying the welfare function, it is assumed that excess demand within each consumer group is rationed according to marginal willingness to pay with costs of doing this proportional to each group's excess demand with per unit costs $\gamma_i \geq 0$, i = 1, 2. The Kuhn-Tucker conditions for optimality for this problem are given as

$$\begin{aligned}\frac{\partial \Psi}{\partial P_{it}} = {} & P_{it} y_{it}'(P_{it}) F\left(\sum_j \overline{X}_{jt} - \sum_i y_{it}(P_{it})\right) \\ & - (a_{jt} + d_{jt}) y_{it}'(P_{it}) F\left(\sum_j \overline{X}_{jt} - \sum y_{it}(P_{it})\right)\end{aligned}$$

$$- \xi_i y_{it}'(P_{it}) \int_{\Sigma_j \overline{X}_{jt} - \Sigma_i y_{it}(P_{it})}^{\infty} \left(\overline{P}_{it} \left\{ y_{it} + \xi_i \left[\sum_j \overline{X}_{jt} - \sum_i y_{it}(P_{it}) \right] \right.\right.$$

$$\left.\left. - \xi_i u_{it} - (a_{jt} + d_{jt}) \right\} \right) dF(u_{it})$$

$$- \xi_k y_{it}'(P_{it}) \int_{\Sigma_j \overline{X}_{jt} - \Sigma_i y_{it}(P_{it})}^{\infty} \left(\overline{P}_{kt} \left\{ y_{kt} + \xi_k \left[\sum_j \overline{X}_{jt} - \sum_i y_{it}(P_{it}) \right] \right.\right.$$

$$\left.\left. - \xi_k u_{kt} - (a_{jt} + d_{jt}) \right\} \right) dF(u_{kt})$$

$$- \left(\sum_i \gamma_{it} \xi_i \right) \left[1 - F\left(\sum_j \overline{X}_{jt} - \sum_i y_{it}(P_{it}) \right) y_{it}'(P_{it}) \right]$$

$$\leq 0 \qquad \text{for } P_{it} \geq 0 \tag{9.18}$$

$$\frac{\partial \Psi}{\partial \overline{X}_{jt}} = \sum_i \xi_i \int_{\Sigma_j \overline{X}_{jt} - \Sigma_i y_{it}(P_{it})}^{\infty} \left(\overline{P}_i \left\{ y_{it} + \xi_i \left[\sum_j \overline{X}_{jt} \right.\right.\right.$$

$$\left.\left.\left. - \sum_i y_{it}(P_{it}) \right] \right\} \right) dF(u_{it}) - b_{jt}$$

$$+ \left(\sum_i \gamma_{it} \xi_i \right) \left[1 - F\left(\sum_j \overline{X}_{it} - \sum_i y_{it}(P_{it}) \right) \right]$$

$$\leq 0 \qquad \text{for } \overline{X}_{jt} \geq 0, \tag{9.19}$$

where F is the cumulative distribution function of the random variable $u_t = \Sigma_i u_{it}$. Note that $F(\Sigma_j \overline{X}_{jt} - \Sigma_i y_{it}(P_{it})) = \Pr(u_t \leq \Sigma_j \overline{X}_{jt} - \Sigma_i y_{it}(P_{it}))$ is just the system reliability.

These optimality conditions are similar to those previously derived for the situation when only a single consumer group was considered. The indication is that for $P_{it} > 0$ and $\overline{X}_{jt} > 0$, price and capacity should be set so that the expected marginal consumer's surplus gains are equated to the expected marginal operating and rationing costs. The third expression of Eq. (9.18) is interpreted as the expected marginal increase in consumer surplus over operating cost for group i from a reduction in price P_{it} slightly when excess demand exists, given that group i is provided with the additional quantity demanded. An analogous interpretation for the fourth term but in the negative direction (i.e., a reduction in consumer's surplus) follows. Consequently, the third and fourth terms in concert represent the difference in net benefits and costs accruing to groups i and k from a reduction in price to group i.

A better appreciation of the results can be obtained if the term $y_{it}(P_{it})$ is deleted (by division) from Eq. (9.18) (assuming, of course, $P_{it} > 0$ and $\overline{X}_{jt} > 0$ and nonzero reliability) and the resulting expression added to Eq. (9.19). The results suggest the optimal price is

$$P_{it} = a_{jt} + d_{jt} + (b_{jt} - \int_{\Sigma_j \overline{X}_{jt} - \Sigma_i y_{it}(P_{it})}^{\infty} P_{it}(y_{it} + \xi_i[\Sigma_j \overline{X}_{jt} - \Sigma_i y_{it}(P_{it})]$$
$$- \xi u_{it} - (a_{jt} + d_{jt}))\, dF(u_{it}))/F(\Sigma_i \overline{X}_{jt} - \Sigma_i y_{it}(P_{it})). \quad (9.20)$$

Optimal capacity is then determined coincidentally with this equation and Eq. (9.19).

The situation when $\xi_i = 0$ is interesting. When all shortages are borne by the other group (i.e., $\xi_i = 0$, $k \neq i$), the price reduces to [from Eq. (9.18)]

$$P_{it} = a_{jt} + d_{jt} + \frac{\gamma_t[1 - F(\Sigma_j \overline{X}_{jt} - \Sigma_i y_{it})]}{F(\Sigma_j \overline{X}_{jt} - \Sigma_i y_{it})}. \quad (9.21)$$

This is similar to the result presented in Eq. (9.13). That is, when one group is not confronted with any shortage arising from a deficiency in capacity, then price is just equal to operating and delivery costs plus a factor reflecting rationing costs.

CONCLUSIONS

In the foregoing analysis, an effort has been made to answer the perplexing question of the impact of demand uncertainty on price. By using a social welfare formulation, a solution is suggested whereby price will approximately equal the cost associated with satisfying the last unit of consumers' demand in a given period. This, in turn, has significant implications for capacity expansion. Namely, capacity is added to keep the risk of failure minimal. As a result, to the extent that the associated costs are higher for the last unit of capacity, a higher price will result. That is, if the marginal capacity has a high operating and delivery cost and low capital cost with high reliability and consequent high total cost (e.g., an internal combustion peaking unit), the indicated result follows. Consequently, there is a direct trade-off between the level of the risk of failure and price. This provides a rationalization for the existence of the price differential between firm and interruptable customers.[7]

NOTES AND REFERENCES

1. G. Brown and M. B. Johnson, "Public Utility Pricing and Output Under Risk." *American Economic Review LIX*(March): 119–128, 1969.
2. R. Turvey, "Public Utility Pricing Under Risk: Comment." *American Economic Review 60*(June): 485–486, 1970.
3. M. L. Visscher, "Welfare Maximizing Price and Output With Stochastic Demand: Comment." *American Economic Review 63*(March): 224–229, 1973.
4. Once again to simplify the exposition, only aggregate demand is considered. This assumption is relaxed in a subsequent section.
5. R. Sherman and M. L. Visscher, "Second Best Pricing With Stochastic Demand." *American Economic Review 68*(March): 41–53, 1978.
6. Ibid.
7. M. A. Crew and P. R. Kleindorfer in *Public Utility Economics* (St. Martins Press, New York, 1979) provide an alternative analysis with comparable conclusions.

Chapter X

Reliability and Regulation in Pricing Public Utility Service

INTRODUCTION

Increasingly, research into the economics of public utility pricing has become focused on the consideration of the efficiency consequences of the regulatory process. (Crew and Kleindorfer[1] have a nice summary of these developments.) This concern with efficiency has led to a much more critical as well as extensive view not only of the nature of efficiency but also of the regulatory process itself. Concern has diverged from the simple neoclassical conditions for efficiency implied by price and marginal cost that are at the center of the early rationale for regulation.[2] The concern now includes the consideration of whether firms are operating at the least cost, the nature of transactions costs, market failure, and the allocative efficiency required in situations where demand and supply are not deterministic (see Crew and Kleindorfer[3]).

The development and implications of the theory of the optimal pricing of public utility service where consumers and producers are spatially diffuse was presented in Chapter III. Starting with a basic neoclassical framework, the setting of peak and off-peak prices by a rate-of-return regulated monopolist was investigated. Among other things, emphasis is placed on how regulation benefitted the peak consumers. This analysis was carried out devoid of any consideration of the effects of stochastic demand. It is the objective of this paper to remedy the situation by explicitly including a rate-of-return consideration when determining the optimal price of public utility service with stochastic demands. This analysis represents an extension of earlier work (Chapter IX) where pricing using social welfare maximization was developed. As before, attention is focused on the electrical energy industry but the results are generally applicable.

A MODEL OF PRICING WITH STOCHASTIC DEMAND

Assume that an economy exists where the demand for electrical energy can be met by many different generating plants. To formulate the understanding and development of the model, the following definitions and notation are introduced.

Let j = generating plants;
t = discrete time periods;
y_{it} = quantity of electrical energy demanded in period t by consumer i;
X_{jt} = quantity of electrical energy generated by plant j in period t;
$\overline{X}_{jt}$ = capacity of plant j in period t;
d_{jt} = delivery cost (transmission and distribution costs) from plant j in period t (assumed to be equal for all consumers);
b_{jt} = cost of capital for an additional unit of generating capacity for plant j in period t;
a_{jt} = operating cost (including fuel cost) for plant j in period t;
r = rate of interest.

Assume, as is typical (Brown and Johnson[4]) that each plant manager knows the aggregate demand function (aggregated across consumers so that $\Sigma_i\, y_{it} = y_t$):

$$y_t(P_t, u_t), \tag{10.1}$$

where u_t is a continuous random variable in period t. Further, it is assumed that the exact form of the continuous probability density function f (u_t) is given. The following properties are attributable to f (u_t).

$$F(Z) = \int_{-\infty}^{z} f(u_t)\, du_t$$

$$\int_{-\infty}^{\infty} u_t f(u_t)\, du_t = 0 \tag{10.2}$$

$$\int_{-\infty}^{\infty} u_t^2\, f(u_t)\, du_t < \infty,$$

where F(Z) defines the probability of $u_t \leq z$. The second expression indicates that first moment (mean) is zero and the last expression denotes that the second moment is finite.

In the subsequent analysis, it will be assumed that the error term is additive. Thus, demand is given by

$$y_t = y_t(P_t) + u_t. \tag{10.3}$$

Given the price there will be a corresponding $y_t(P_t)$ to which will be added a random term. Consequently, for actual sales of electrical energy in period t,

$$Q_t = \begin{cases} y_t(P_t) + u_t & u_t \leq \sum_i \overline{X}_{it} - y_t(P_t) \\ \overline{X}_t & u_t > \sum_i \overline{X}_{it} - y_t(P_t). \end{cases} \tag{10.4}$$

If actual demand is less than generating capacity, then the quantity demanded will exactly be equal to actual sales. If for the given price, however, a value of u_t should occur such that $y_t(P_t, u_t)$ is greater than capacity, actual sales cannot exceed capacity although demand potentially can.

Before extending the results of the previous analysis, it is useful to recapitulate them. The basic model under certainty envisages a profit-maximizing firm subject to the constraint that the rate of return the firm earns on its capital stock be no greater than some prespecified level set by the regulatory commission. The results obtained for this case are that such a regulated firm will use an inefficiently large amount of capital at the output level it chooses. Nevertheless, for some allowed rates of return, social welfare increases over the unregulated monopoly situation. Indeed, as the allowed rate of return decreases from the unregulated monopoly level, output increases while the magnitude of factor input (i.e., capital) distortions from cost-minimizing levels increases. Finding an optimal allowed rate of return then consists of weighing consumer benefits from increased output against the social costs of increased supply inefficiencies.

Under uncertainty, there are a variety of possibilities for extending this analysis. These include such issues as whether the regulator sets the price (consistent with the determined fair rate of return), or whether the regulated firm sets any price it wishes consistent with the allowed rate of return; whether price is set before or after demand uncertainty is revealed; whether the rate-of-return constraint is required to hold with certainty ex post, or whether it is required to hold in an expected value sense ex ante; and whether demand must be met or whether excess demand is allowed.

In constructing a model for the pricing of public utility service these are some of the factors that should be answered. It is to this model we now turn.

A MODEL OF PROFIT MAXIMIZATION

Assume that the electric utility (hereafter, the firm) has as its objective the maximization of expected profit. The problem may be stated as follows. Maximize expect profit Π:

$$\begin{aligned} \Pi = \sum_t \sigma^{t-1}[\overline{P}_t(y_t - u_t)y_t(P_t)] \\ - \sum_j (a_{jt} + d_{jt})y_t(P_t) \\ - \sum_j b_{jt}\overline{X}_{jt}, \end{aligned} \tag{10.5}$$

where $\overline{P}_t$ is the inverse demand function possessing the necessary regularity properties (e.g., $\partial\overline{P}_t/\partial y_t < 0$) and $\sigma^{t-1} = 1/(1 + r)^{t-1}$.

The Kuhn-Tucker conditions for the saddle value problem (in the case of the profit maximizer) are well known to be

$$\frac{\partial \Pi}{\partial P_t} = [P_t y_t'(P_t) + y_t(P_t)]F\left(\sum_j \overline{X}_{jt} - y_t(P_t)\right)$$

$$- (a_{jt} + d_{jt})y_t'(P_t)F\left(\sum_j \overline{X}_{jt} - y_t(P_t)\right)$$

$$\leq 0 \qquad \text{for } P_t \geq 0. \tag{10.6}$$

$$\frac{\partial \Pi}{\partial \overline{X}_{jt}} = \sum_t \int_{\Sigma_j \overline{X}_{jt} - y_t(P_t)}^{\infty} f(u_t)\left[\overline{P}\left(\sum_j \overline{X}_{jt} - u_t\right)\right.$$

$$\left. - (a_{jt} + d_{jt})\right] dF(u_t) - b_{jt}$$

$$\leq 0 \qquad \text{for } \overline{X}_j \geq 0, \tag{10.7}$$

where, as before, f is the density function and F is the cumulative distribution function of the random variable u_t. Note in passing that since $F(\hat{u}_t) = \Pr(u_t \leq \hat{u}_t)$ by the definition of a cumulative distribution (Pr denotes probability),

$$F\left(\sum_j \overline{X}_{jt} - y_t(P_t)\right) = \Pr\left(u_t \leq \sum_j \overline{X}_{jt} - y_t(P_t)\right)$$

$$= \Pr\left(y_t(P_t) + t \leq \sum_j \overline{X}_{jt}\right)$$

is simply the reliability in period t. If $P_t > 0$ and if reliability is nonzero, then from Eq. (10.6),

$$P_t y_t'(P_t) + y_t(P_t) = (a_{jt} + d_{jt})y_t'(P_t), \tag{10.8}$$

where implicitly plant j is the last to be brought on line (i.e., the combined operating and delivery costs for this plant exceed those of all other plants). Note that the expression on the left-hand-side of Eq. (10.8) is just the marginal revenue in period t, MR_t.

To interpret this condition in a meaningful way it is necessary to rewrite Eq. (10.8) as follows:

$$P_t\left(1 + \frac{1}{\varepsilon_t}\right) = a_{jt} + d_{jt}, \tag{10.8a}$$

where ε_t is the elasticity of demand defined as $(dy_t/dP_t)(P_t/y_t)$. Since the demand functions were assumed to be well behaved, the second term in parenthesis on the left-hand side is negative so that price will exceed marginal operating cost plus delivery cost. Note that the expression on the left hand side is nothing more than the marginal revenue. Thus, in this setting the neoclassical result obtains whereby marginal revenue equals marginal cost.

It is possible that reliability is zero so that deleting the expression $F(\Sigma_j \overline{X}_{jt} - y(P_t))$ is not justified. While the interpretation of the Kuhn-Tucker conditions are not as straightforward as before, they do have an economic meaning. Specifically, the marginal loss in revenue in excess of variable cost (operating cost and delivery cost) in period t from not increasing capacity slightly is $\overline{P}(\Sigma_j \overline{X}_{jt} - u_t) - (a_{jt} + d_{jt})$ if capacity is exceeded and zero otherwise. Thus, Eq. (10.7) says set $\Sigma_j \overline{X}_{jt}$ just large enough so that marginal expected losses due to unmet demand are equal to marginal capacity cost b_{jt}. To do this when uncertainty is small or capacity cost large would generally require the peak price to exceed $a_{jt} + d_{jt}$.

THE RATIONING COST AND RATE-OF-RETURN REGULATION

For the objective function [Eq. (10.5)] to accurately measure profit, it is necesary to assume that in the event of the quantity demanded exceeding capacity, consumers will be ranked according to their willingness to pay. The presumption is that this process is not costless. In the spirit of Sherman and Visscher[5] and Visscher[6] in the event of scarcity, costs are incurred in ensuring that consumers are rationed in accordance with their marginal willingness to pay. For a utility employing a two-part tariff, for example, negotiations might occur between the electric utility and its consumers whereby it agrees to pay in some sense (e.g., through a reduction in rates) those consumers who will be cut off in the event that the quantity demanded exceeds capacity. While the present analysis is devoid of such a scheme, the contention is that there are costs in rationing according to the willingness to pay in the event of excess demand. Additionally, as the magnitude of excess demand increases, it is likely that the transactions costs from dealing with consumers, when viewed from the electric utility's perspective, will increase. Consequently, the sum of such costs when the quantity demanded exceeds capacity is

$$R = \sum_t \gamma_t \left[y_t(P_t) + u_t - \sum_j \overline{X}_{jt} \right], \tag{10.9}$$

where γ_t is the rationing cost incurred whenever capacity is exceeded and wherever it is monotonically increasing, convex, and differentiable. Now introduce a regulatory constraint which limits profit at or below some level which will generally increase as the size of the system is increased. Specifically, the rate-of-return criterion holds the firm's earnings at or below a fixed amount, θ, for installed capacity. This translates into

$$\Pi_t \leq \theta\left(\sum_j \overline{X}_{jt} \right), \tag{10.10}$$

where Π_t is the expected profit in period t. If it is assumed that the firm maximizes expected profit, then combining the rationing cost and the rate-of-return constraint with the previous objective function (profit function), the value to be maximized becomes

$$\Pi^*(\Pi, \gamma, \theta) = \Pi - \sum_t \gamma_t \left[y_t(P_t) + u_t - \sum_j \overline{X}_{jt} \right]$$

$$+ \sum_t \rho_t \left(\theta \sum_j \overline{X}_{jt} - \Pi_t \right) \tag{10.11}$$

where ρ_t is just the quasi-rent accruing to the utility by adding an additional unit of generating capacity (i.e., the marginal profitability of an additional unit of capacity). Following the previous procedure, the expected value of Eq. (10.11) is maximized. The Kuhn-Tucker conditions are given as

$$\frac{\partial \Pi^*}{\partial P_t} = (1 - \rho_t)[P_t y'(P_t) + g(P_t)]F\left(\sum_j \overline{X}_{jt} - y_t(P_t) \right)$$

$$- (a_{jt} + d_{jt}) y_t'(P_t) F\left(\sum_j \overline{X}_{jt} - y_t(P_t) \right)$$

$$- \gamma_t \left[1 - F\left(\sum_j \overline{X}_{jt} - y_t(P_t) \right) \right] y_t'(P_t)$$

$$\leq 0 \qquad \text{for } P_t \geq 0 \tag{10.12}$$

$$\frac{\partial \Pi^*}{\partial \overline{X}_{jt}} = (1 - \rho_t) \int_{\Sigma_j \overline{X}_{jt} - y_t(P_t)}^{\infty} f(u_t) \left[\overline{P}\left(\sum_j \overline{X}_{jt} - u_t \right) - (a_{jt} + d_{jt}) \right] dF(u_t)$$

$$- (1 - \rho_t) b_{jt} + \gamma_t \left[1 - F\left(\sum_j \overline{X}_{jt} - y_t(P_t) \right) \right] + \rho_t \theta$$

$$\leq 0 \qquad \text{for } \overline{X}_{jt} \geq 0. \tag{10.13}$$

When reliability is nonzero and $P_t > 0$, dividing through by $F(\Sigma_j \overline{X}_{jt} - y_t(P_t))$ yields

$$P_t\left(1 + \frac{1}{\varepsilon_t}\right) = (a_{jt} + d_{jt}) + \frac{\gamma_t[1 - F(\Sigma_j \overline{X}_{jt} - y_t(P_t))]}{(1 - \rho_t)F(\Sigma_j \overline{X}_{jt} - y_t(P_t))}, \tag{10.14}$$

where again ε_t is the elasticity of demand, and implicity plant j is the last to be brought on line. Thus, marginal revenue is set equal to the sum of marginal operating, delivery, and rationing costs but it is also a function of reliability and the quasi-rent ρ_t. A determination of the optimal level of reliability is obtained by using Eq. (10.13). This indicates that, for $\overline{X}_{jt} \geq 0$, the reserve margin $\Sigma_j \overline{X}_{jt} - y_t(P_t)$ should be set so the marginal cost of capacity equals the sum of the expected marginal rationing cost, the reduction in profit, and the marginal value (quasi-rent) of an additional unit of plant capacity.

Now if it is assumed that the losses in profit [the first term on the right-hand side of Eq. (10.13)] are negligible (this is assumed for ease of exposition in what follows), then the marginal cost of capacity is

$$b_{jt} = \frac{\gamma_t[1 - F(\Sigma_j \overline{X}_{jt} - y_t(P_t))]}{1 - \rho_t} + \frac{\rho_t \theta}{1 - \rho_t} \tag{10.15}$$

or

$$1 - F\left(\sum_j \overline{X}_{jt} - y_t(P_t) \right) = (1 - \rho_t)\left(\frac{b_{jt}}{\gamma_t} - \rho_t \theta \right). \tag{10.15a}$$

This says that the ratio of the marginal capacity cost (if, implicitly, the last plant brought on line) to the marginal rationing cost minus the marginal value of an additional unit of capacity adjusted by one minus the quasi-rent of the additional unit of capacity determines the optimal level of reliability. Further, combining this with Eq. (10.12) and assuming $P_t > 0$, then

$$P_t\left(1 + \frac{1}{\varepsilon_t}\right) = a_{jt} + d_{jt} + \left(b_{jt} - \frac{\rho_t\theta}{F(\Sigma_j \overline{X}_{jt} - y_t(P_t))}\right). \qquad (10.16)$$

The implication of this is that if the error term has the characteristics previously attributed to it, Eq. (10.15a) defines the level of $\overline{X}_{jt}$ such that the probability of failure to meet demand (1 minus the level of reliability) is less than a specified level for the optimally determined price. Further, the level of reliability has a larger impact on marginal revenue than is explicitly represented in Eq. (10.16). In particular, capacity expansion plans will be adjusted so that Eq. (10.15) is satisfied. This will necessarily yield a higher level of capacity the greater the desired level of reliability. Since capacity is installed and brought into use on the basis of merit ordering (i.e., in increasing order of cost), marginal revenue, and hence prices, will be set to this higher value. Thus, de facto, both are coincidentally determined. That is, if one is given the capacity cost (and hence the level of capacity), then the level of reliability and the marginal revenue are determined. Alternatively, given the reliability level, both the capacity level and marginal revenue are known.

Finally if attention is focused on the impact of regulation through the rate-of-return constraint, it can be seen that regulation will result in a lowering of the price from the profit maximization level so long as capacity additions are positive. This will happen because the quasi-rent of an additional unit of capacity will be positive (given that $P_t > 0$ and $\theta > 0$). With a lower quasi-rent, total marginal costs [the left-hand side of Eq. (10.16)] will be adjusted downward. Equating marginal revenue to this lower marginal cost results in a large output at a lower price. Thus, the regulator achieves the goal that output is increased from the profit-maximization level.

It is possible that this adjusted marginal cost will be sufficiently lower that capacity will be larger than the level required were price equated to actual marginal cost. If this occurs, one is observing the Averch–Johnson effect.[7] There will be an overbuilding of capacity because profits increase with the level of generating capacity. The firm will pass along the benefits of regulation to those consumers whose increased demand causes an increase in capacity.

The expansion of capacity and the magnitude of the fair rate of return θ are related in a predictable way. Namely, the closer the fair rate is to the cost of capital, the larger will be the capacity. This can be seen by observing that the quasi-rent of the marginal unit of capacity is lower the closer the cost of capital is to the rate of return, and thus by Eq. (10.16) the indicated result holds.

CONCLUSION

The principal question addressed in the foregoing analysis concerned the optimal price profile for a regulated public utility where demand is stochastic. Through the introduction of rationing costs and a rate-of-return constraint, marginal revenue will be approximately equated to the cost associated with satisfying the last unit of consumers' demand. This has significant implications for capacity expansion. Namely, capacity is added to keep the risk of failure minimal. As a result, to the extent that the associated costs are higher for the last unit of capacity, a higher marginal revenue and hence price will result. That is, if the marginal unit of capacity has a high operating and delivery cost and low capital cost with high reliability and consequent high total cost (e.g., an internal combustion peaking unit), the indicated result follows. Consequently, there is a direct tradeoff between the level of risk of failure and marginal revenue. This provides a rationalization for the existence of the price differential between firm and interruptible customers. Finally, if the firm is constrained to earn a fair return on its capital investment, it will set prices to favor the consumers generating the expansion in capacity.

NOTES AND REFERENCES

1. M. A. Crew and P. R. Kleindorfer, *Public Utility Economics*. New York: St. Martins Press, 1979.
2. R. Turvey, "Public Utility Pricing and Output Under Risk: Comment." *American Economic Review 60*(June): 485–486, 1970.
3. M. A. Crew and P. R. Kleindorfer, "Peak Load Pricing with a Diverse Technology." *The Bell Journal of Economics* (Spring): 207–231, 1976.

4. G. Brown and M. B. Johnson, "Public Utility Pricing and Output Under Risk." *American Economic Review 59*(March): 119–128, 1969.
5. R. Sherman and M. L. Visscher, "Second Best Pricing with Stochastic Demand." *American Economic Review 68*(March): 41–53, 1978.
6. M. L. Visscher, "Welfare Maximizing Price and Output with Stochastic Demand: Comment." *American Economic Review 63*(March): 224–229, 1973.
7. H. Averch and L. Johnson, "Behavior of the Firm Under Regulatory Constraint." *American Economic Review 52*(December): 1053–1069, 1962.

Chapter XI

Conclusion

GENERAL CONSIDERATIONS

The optimal pricing of electrical energy implies a rate structure such that the cost to any consumer of changing the pattern or level of their consumption equals the cost to the electric utility of meeting the consumer's demand. This can be achieved more or less closely according to the behavioral assumptions of both consumers and producers that are used to determine this optimal price. The preceding chapters have explored the most important of these behavioral assumptions and endeavored to develop consistent pricing rules. It is useful to summarize these assumptions and pricing rules and extract the thread of commonality running through the various models.

Of central importance in approaching the peak-load pricing problem has been with a more exact representation of the spatial considerations of demand and supply. In this context on the supply side, focus on individual plants is a natural way to look at the technology involved in the generation of electrical energy. With the relaxation of the assumption of homogeneous generating capacity (characteristic of the early work of Boiteux and Steiner as noted in the first chapter) and with the recognition of the fact that the efficient satisfaction of a periodic (temporally varying) demand will generally imply a mix of different types of capacity with different operating and investment costs, the first chapters offer a significant departure from the way the problem has been investigated historically.

This approach gives considerable emphasis to the calculation of the marginal costs of providing service to meet a set of demands in the context of a heterogeneous production technology and the optimal utilization of the spatially diffuse generating plants. It also recognizes that generating capacity is not available at some periods (for example, because of periodic maintenance) and that, consequently, the identification of peak and off-peak periods depends inexorably on both the fluctuations in demand and the fluctuations in capacity availability due to maintenance requirements.

Next, demand considerations are explicitly represented. Thus, there is the recognition that demands in each period are responsive to price and that a demand period which appears to be, say, the peak period, when all users are charged identical prices may no longer be a unique peak period when efficient prices are charged. This problem recognizes the true joint cost situation. Only when the off-peak load fails to use plant to its maximum extent when priced at marginal cost equal to operating cost plus delivery cost does the peak-load bear the entire burden of capacity costs. Otherwise, each such period must bear some of the marginal capacity costs.

There are other conclusions which are critical for our understanding about turning knowledge of demand and the costs of supply into actual electrical energy prices. First, there is the explicit recognition of the fact that electrical energy demands are not only periodic but also highly uncertain. This uncertainty leads to the possibility that demand will exceed available capacity at times. This latter possibility means that loads will have to be occasionally curtailed. The uncertainty associated with both demand and supply (forced outages) is what requires the carrying of reserve margins for electric utility generating systems.

Second, there is the realization that curtailment costs or rationing costs are incurred when an uncertain system requires, on occasion, some loads to be curtailed. The introduction of such rationing costs in the context of uncertainty has implications for both investment planning and pricing. On the investment side, rationing costs and the ability to reduce or increase them on the margin by increasing or decreasing the level of capacity leads to rules that determine the optimal levels of capacity and the associated reserve margins. In the most elementary situation, capacity is expanded up to the point at which the cost of an additional unit of capacity is equal to the expected marginal rationing cost. On the pricing side, this recognition leads to optimal pricing rules which set prices equal to expected marginal operating and delivery costs plus expected marginal rationing cost for each relevant demand period. By using the equilibrium conditions for the optimal amount of capacity, the expected rationing cost figure can be expressed as some proportion of the marginal capacity cost, so that prices in general reflect both expected marginal costs plus a capacity cost component. Since the marginal rationing cost for the different periods are essentially determined by the intensities of demand in each period, this procedure gives similar results to those in the treatment of the joint cost aspects of the shifting peak problem, but in the context of demand and supply uncertainty.

Finally, while much of the treatment of variable load pricing of electrical energy deals with the generation system and the heterogeneous technology associated with it, further consideration has been given to the transmission and distribution systems, costs of which may be as much as 30 percent of the total cost of supplying electrical energy. In particular it is recognized that while the generation and transmission systems are in a sense "common" systems and that marginal costs reflect system load characteristics, as one moves through the distribution system to the point of end use, the system becomes more and more "individual." This implies that while the nature of the cost causality for common system components implies peak-load prices based on system load characteristics, the costs of the distribution system depends on individual characteristics or the demand characteristics of particular groups of customers which is not necessarily coincident with system demand patterns.

All things considered, the models developed here indicate that the application of marginal-cost pricing principles to the actual calculation of prices is considerably more complicated than simple prescriptions, based on useful but simple models, might indicate. Considerations of demand and its reponsiveness to price variations, uncertainty, rationing costs, heterogeneous technology, and other complications of an actual supply system help to extend the basic principles to incorporate additional considerations that more accurately reflect reality.

IMPLICATIONS OF RELIABILITY

One final comment is necessary to underscore the complexity of the relationship between reliability and regulation. This comment is made in the context of the models developed in Chapters IX and X.

Even if reserve margins increase as regulation becomes tighter, such increases may not be undesirable from a welfare point of view. Indeed, as rationing becomes more costly or more inefficient, it is clear that welfare optimal reliability approaches unity, and this is so for any fixed price. Since the unregulated firm sets reliability strictly between 0 and 1, one sees that, for sufficiently high rationing or shortage costs, the unregulated monopoly will have a lower reserve margin than is socially desirable. Thus, the increases in reserve margin occasioned by decreasing the allowed rate of return below that which an unregulated monopoly would achieve may be all to the good.

Suppose, however, that a regulatory commission is faced with an excess capacity problem in that there is a gross divergence between actual reserve margin and the reserve margin which, at existing prices, would be implied by the welfare optimal capacity condition. It is tempting to argue that the commission should simply attempt to restrict (regulate) reliability level or reserve margin in this case. There are problems, however, with this. First, there are severe informational difficulties in translating an allowed reliability level or reserve margin constraint into an actual capacity and operating regime because of the problem of maintenance and availability of plants. Specifically, if commissions employed a "used-and-useful" criterion to say that particular plants were in excess of what was required to provide a regulated level of reliability, the utilities could overcome this by reducing maintenance, causing more plant downtime and therefore more use of previously "unused and unuseful" plants. The only cure for this would appear to be more regulation, now of maintenance.

Somewhere in this increasing spiral of regulatory intervention, one would expect the social costs of regulation to exceed its benefits. At the risk of contributing to this spiral, the results of these chapters would seem nevertheless to call for a more explicit treatment of reliability and reserve margin in regulatory proceedings. This will require a more positive approach to reliability than has been apparent in theory or practice to date.[1]

The initial element of a positive approach to reliability and regulation would be the recognition by both the electric utility industry and regulatory commissions of the importance of developing benchmarks for reliability and reserve margins. This is not likely to be an easy task, even given the trust in the theoretical models addressed to this issue. One problem is that we have very little experience in assessing the rationing costs and surplus losses associated with excess demand; these data are required for the welfare-optimal benchmark developed.

There are also substantial differences in reserve margins among public utilities, suggesting that a closer scrutiny of reliability and reserve margins by commissions is called for. A simple proposal might be for commissions, when they have reason to believe that reserve margins of a particular firm are excessive, to move to exclude some plant from the rate base. Clearly the process by which these moves and supporting audits are undertaken must be structured with great care.

Taking account of the incentives toward increasing reserve margins as rate of return is reduced, which the theoretical models suggest, one would expect that the societal optimum might dictate some inverse relationship between allowed rate of return and reserve margin, both as a descriptive and normative position.

NOTE AND REFERENCE

1. This is the suggestion of M. A. Crew and P. R. Kleindorfer in "Some Elementary Considerations of Reliability and Regulation." In *Problems in Public Utility Economics and Regulation.* Lexington, Mass.: D.C. Heath and Company, 1979.

Index